PRINCIPLES FOR PRESENTING

THE PURITY

OF THE PASSAGE

By

Pastor D.L. Richardson, Ph.D.

(501) 758-1525

ISBN: 1-933594-32-2

Printed in the United States of America

WITH GRATITUDE

I want to first of all thank God for counting me worthy to be called to the proclamation ministry and entrusting me with the responsibility of preaching and teaching His Word. I also want to thank the many friends who helped to make this publication possible. They include Dr. Bill Sheffield of Louisiana Baptist Theological Seminary, Shreveport, LA, Faith Baptist Church Publications, the members of First Baptist Church Main Street, North Little Rock, AR, and my lovely companion for life, Tammy.

This book is gratefully dedicated to my beautiful gift from God, my daughter Alicia, and the late Vada C. Sanders, my mother.

CONTENTS

Preface

The purpose of this writing is to equip, encourage, and empower those who are students and sharers of the Word of God through teaching and preaching to maintain the message and meaning that the Master is manifesting throughout the manual known as the Bible. It is my prayer that this material will help to sharpen your learning and shape your life as you sup from the living Word of God.

Principles for Presenting the Purity of the Passage is a resource tool for those who are seasoned and those who are starting in the proclamation ministry. You will discover as you allow the Spirit of God to minister to you that this can be a vital and valuable instrument of information and inspiration. These principles will yield the following benefits:

1. The revelation of the message intended by God in the Bible
2. The reliable proclamation of the Word based on scriptural truth
3. A reservoir of preaching and teaching material
4. The reconstruction of the preacher/teacher as a pupil of the Word

5. The rise of knowledge, wisdom, and understanding for the student

6. The research of the Word in a comprehensive pattern

7. The redirecting of a thought process

8. The resources to tackle hard-to-interpret texts

9. A refuge against the insertion of false ideology.

10. A routine of study that will aid in avoiding ruts and pet topics.

It is a great honor and privilege to be trusted by God as a preacher/teacher of His Word; however; with this honor and privilege comes an awesome responsibility. James speaks of the severer judgment for presenters of the Word (James 3:1). Scripture reveals that Moses and Aaron experienced a more severe judgment in that because of one act of disobedience they forfeited their entrance into the Promised Land. The task and the responsibility is an awesome one.

Presenting the purity of the passage will require the presenter to perform a close investigation of the passage being studied. The presenter must not be satisfied with just scraping the surface of the Scripture. There must be a willingness to dig deep to the root of the passage to ensure a truthful presentation of the Word of God. As you discover these helpful principles, it is my prayer that the Spirit of God will grant you the will and the wisdom to apply them to the preaching/teaching ministry that has been entrusted in your care as you make full proof of your ministry.

Chapter One

The Presentation of the Problem

"The Heresy"

The apostle Paul in the second of two inspired letters he wrote to his son in the faith Timothy, states that "the time will come when they will not endure sound doctrine, but according to their own desires, because they have itching ears, they will heap up for themselves teachers; and they will turn their ears away from the truth, and be turned aside to fables."[1] I want to submit to you that the time has arrived and not only does the hearer have itching ears, but the herald has loose lips. The congregation is itching for entertainment and the clergy is itching to entertain. The trainee is itching for a pleasant sensation and the teacher is itching to produce the sensation. The problem is the perversion of the truth. Twisted teaching and parody preaching is destroying the lives of the listeners and God is going to hold the purveyor of His truth accountable. James admonishes many not to become teachers because of the stricter judgment. (James 3:1). Regardless of the

---

[1] *The Holy Bible: King James Version.* 1995. Logos Research Systems, Inc.: Oak Harbor, WA

11

lack of education or lack of skill, the messenger is responsible for presenting the purity of the passage and not heretical doctrine.

The absence of sound preaching and teaching is directly related to an erosion of confidence in the authority and sufficiency of Scripture. At the beginning of the nineteenth century the battle lines were drawn against the forces of liberalism. Liberals were challenging the miraculous, questioning the divine, and opposing the historicity of the New Testament documents. Evangelicals weathered that storm, and empty liberal churches testify to the futility of the liberal quest for a demythologized Christ. But today the battle is more subtle. The Scriptures are neglected and debased and are used only as a springboard for all kinds of "talks" that are far removed from genuine biblical exposition.

It is very possible to attend a service of worship in an avowedly evangelical congregation and find that if the Bible is read or referred to at all (and there is no guarantee it will be), it is weightless in its influence because of inadequate presentation or emphasis. There is little, if any, sense of either the preacher or the congregation bowing under the majestic authority of God's written Word. We live at a time when being unsure and vague is in vogue. There is a contemporary distrust of anything or anyone who is assured or authoritative. Young pastors particularly may find themselves intimidated in such an environment and begin to preach sermons that have their genesis in what people want to hear rather than in what God has chosen to say and command.

Presenting the purity of the passage is also undermined by a fascination with the so-called extra-biblical "prophetic word." Preachers and teachers now will read from the Scriptures, then close Bible and preface their remarks with "This is what God is saying to us now." When the presenter does this, he is taking the risk of diverting the listener away from a clear reliance and revelation on the sufficiency of Scripture.

Sinclair B. Ferguson wrote of such preaching, "While it is denied that additions are being made to the canon of Scripture, it is nevertheless implied that an actual addition is being made to the canon of living. Otherwise the illumination of Scripture and the wisdom to apply it would be sufficient." [2]

One of the reasons for the disinterest and drifting away of sound doctrine is because the presenters are lifeless, dull, and even thoroughly boring. One can never cease to be amazed by the ingenuity and initiative of some preachers and teachers who are capable of taking the powerful, life-changing text of Scripture and communicating it with all the passion of someone reading aloud from the Yellow Pages!

---

[2] *The Holy Spirit,* Downers Grove, Ill.: InterVarsity Press, 1996, p. 231).

Calvin said of God's work in preaching, "He deigns to consecrate the mouths and tongues of men to his service, making his own voice to be heard in them. Whenever God is pleased to bless their labor, he makes their doctrine efficacious by the power of his Spirit; and the voice, which is in itself mortal, is made an instrument to communicate eternal life." [3]

The expositor is God's servant, submitting to and proclaiming the text of Holy Writ. The passage itself should be looked upon as the voice, the speech of God and should be presented in the same manner. The expositor is not a poet moving his listeners by rhythm and rhyme. He is a *herald* speaking by the strength and authority of the Holy Spirit the whole counsel of God who seeks to avoid the disease of defiling the presentation of the Word.

The preventive medicine for this disease is the precise preaching and truthful teaching of the Word of God.

"The Hope"

What makes a good preacher and good teacher? Well, a number of things can easily be echoed: reverence for the Master,

---

[3] *Pulpit and People*, Nigel M. Cameron and Sinclair B. Ferguson, editors [Edinburgh: Rutherford House, 1986].

respect for the ministry, love for the pew, loyalty to the pulpit, good meditation, good memory, and good material—all these are essential, but not enough. The preacher/teacher must be able to effectively handle the Word of God with accuracy. The hope is to develop a continuous generation of presenters of the Word that will truthfully teach and precisely preach the whole counsel of God.

It is important that the presenter of the Word of God understand the following attributes about the Book that he is preaching or teaching from known- as the Bible as he seeks to present the purity of the passage:

1. The infallibility of the Bible

The Bible, in its entirety, has no mistakes. Specifically, in its original autographs it is without errors. In Psalm 19:7 the Bible says of itself, "The law of the Lord is perfect." It is flawless because it was authored by God—and He is flawless. Therefore, if God wrote the Bible, and if He is the ultimate authority, and if His character is flawless, then the Bible is flawless and is the ultimate authority. You see, the fact that God is perfect demands that the original autograph, the original giving of the Word of God, must also be perfect. So, the Bible is infallible, and that's the first reason to study it; it is the only Book that never makes a mistake—everything it says is the truth.

15

2.   The inerrancy of the Bible

The Bible is not only infallible in totality, but inerrant in its parts. In Proverbs 30:5–6 it says, "Every word of God is pure.... Add thou not unto his words, lest he reprove thee, and thou be found a liar." So every Word of God is pure and true. There is no need to neither add to what God has already stated nor subtract from it because the truth is the truth as presented by the God. He is the only authority.

3.   The inclusiveness of the Bible

The Bible is complete within itself and nothing needs to be added. There exists a philosophy/theology combination known as neo-orthodoxy. It tells us that the Bible was simply a comment in its day on man's spiritual experiences, and today man is still having spiritual experiences, therefore he needs another comment. One writer said that "we need a Bible to be written today, just as we did when the Bible we have in our hands was written, because we need somebody to comment on what God is doing now. Today when Tom or Mary stands up in your church and says, 'Thus says the Lord,' they are as equally inspired as Isaiah, Jeremiah, or any of the other prophets." [4] In other words, they claim that the Bible is not complete. That's the current philosophical/theological

---

[4] J. Rodman Williams, *The Era of the Spirit*, Logos International, 1971.

thought. Let's look at the end of the last book of the Bible, Revelation 22:18b-19 states, "If any man shall add unto these things, God shall add unto him the plagues that are written in this book; and if any man shall take away from the words of the book of this prophecy, God shall take away his part from the tree of life, and out of the holy city, and from the things which are written in this book." [5] The Bible ends with a warning not to take away anything, and not to add anything. That's a testimony of its completeness. It is *infallible* in its portion, *inerrant* in its parts, and it is *inclusive* in its presentation.

4.   The influence of the Bible

The Bible is the final authority. Isaiah 1:2 says, "Hear, O heavens, and give ear, O earth; for the Lord hath spoken." [6] Whatever God says is the final word and He should be heard when He speaks. It is the truth because it comes from the true God.

5.   The introduction of the Bible

---

[5] *The Holy Bible: King James Version.* 1995. Logos Research Systems, Inc.: Oak Harbor, WA
[6] *The Holy Bible: King James Version.* 1995. Logos Research Systems, Inc.: Oak Harbor, WA

How did we get the Bible? Harper shares the following discussion concerning the formation of the Bible. "The English word 'Bible' is derived from the Old French *bible,* which is in turn based on Latin *biblia* and Greek *biblia* ('books'), plural of *biblion,* diminutive from *biblos.*" This is a term that generally refers to the Scriptures of the Christian church, but it may also denote the canon of Jewish scriptures.

The Bible has been conferred to us in many forms. *The Hebrew Bible,* often called the Masoretic Text (MT), is an anthology of twenty-four books written in Hebrew (but including also a few passages in Aramaic). Its form is as follows:

(1)　　The Law (Heb. = torah): Genesis, Exodus, Leviticus, Numbers, Deuteronomy (the Pentateuch)

(2)　　The Prophets (Heb. = nebi'im):

(A)　　Former Prophets: Joshua, Judges, Samuel (1 & 2), Kings (1 & 2)

(B)　　Latter Prophets: Isaiah, Jeremiah, Ezekiel; Hosea, Joel, Amos, Obadiah, Jonah, Micah, Nahum, Habakkuk, Zephaniah, Haggai, Zechariah, Malachi)

(3)　　The Writings (Heb. = ketubim):

18

(A)   Poetical Books: Psalms, Job, Proverbs,

(B)   Five Rolls: Ruth, Song of Solomon, Ecclesiastes, Lamentations, Esther,

(C)   Historical Books: Daniel, Ezra-Nehemiah, Chronicles (1 & 2).

A translation of the Jewish scriptures into Greek, commonly labeled the *Septuagint* (LXX), probably had its earliest form as a translation of the Pentateuch into Greek in the third century B.C. This anthology included not only the books of the Hebrew Bible listed above, but also a number of other writings (although there are variations in the manuscripts): 1 Esdras, the Wisdom of Solomon, the Wisdom of Jesus, the Son of Sirach (Ecclesiasticus), Judith, Tobit, Baruch, the Letter of Jeremiah, the four books of Maccabees, plus certain additions to books in the MT- notably the additions to Daniel (Susanna, Bel and the Dragon, the Prayer of Azariah, and the Song of the Three Young Men)- and to the book of Esther.

The Christian Bible consists of the Old Testament (OT) and the New Testament (NT). In the Roman Catholic and Eastern Christian communities (e.g., Greek, Syriac, Armenian), the OT is based on the LXX, while most Protestant churches accept only the books of the Hebrew Bible as their OT canon. The NT canon we

19

have inherited now consists of twenty-seven books: the Gospels of Matthew, Mark, Luke, John; Acts of the Apostles; Romans, 1 and 2 Corinthians, Galatians, Ephesians, Philippians, Colossians, 1 and 2 Thessalonians, 1 and 2 Timothy, Titus, Philemon (all attributed to Paul); Hebrews, James, 1 and 2 Peter, 1, 2, and 3 John, Jude, and Revelation.

Introduction of the Biblical Canons: The development of the various biblical canons was a long and complex process. Prior to the fall of Jerusalem in A.D. 70, the working canon of Jewish scriptures in Palestine seems to have been rather open-ended and inclusive. After 70 A.D., however, there was a narrowing tendency, so that by about the time of the Council of Jamnia (ca. A.D. 90) the rabbis had rejected the larger canon that continued in the LXX in favor of the twenty-four-book collection we have labeled the Hebrew Bible. Ultimately this Jamnian canon became the canon for Judaism as a whole.

We are unable to reconstruct with confidence precisely which lists of books were considered authoritative by Jesus and His earliest followers. By the second century, it was not uncommon to find church fathers using books found in the LXX but not in the Jamnian canon. Yet a few writers (e.g., Origen, Jerome) distinguished between the books of the Hebrew Bible and the remainder in the LXX tradition; indeed, the latter group they labeled

'Apocrypha' ('hidden' or 'outside' books), a group they considered edifying but not authoritative. On the whole, however, Eastern and Roman Catholic tradition generally considered the OT 'apocryphal' books to be canonical. It was not until the Protestant Reformation that these books were clearly denied canonical status (in Protestant circles). The Roman church, however, continues to affirm their place in the canon of Scripture.

The history of the NT canon is one of intricacy and irregularity. All of the currently accepted NT books achieved early acknowledgment in some circles; however, no canonical lists appear before around A.D. 150, when the heretic Marcion proclaimed a canon consisting of his version of Luke and ten Letters of Paul. By the end of the century, more inclusive lists of authoritative NT writings were advanced, e.g., the Muratorian Canon (listing at least twenty-two of our present twenty-seven); Irenaeus, a bishop of Lyon in the mid-second century A.D. (clearly naming twenty-one); and Tertullian, a North African presbyter of the same period (twenty-two). The inclusion of Revelation was a matter of considerable disagreement. The second and third Letters of John, 2 Peter, and Jude were often excluded, and Hebrews was sometimes omitted. At the same time, writings not found presently in our canon of twenty-seven were sometimes cited. The twenty-seven-book Latin Vulgate (Vg.) of Jerome (late fourth century) exerted considerable influence upon what books were generally

21

recognized; moreover, provincial church councils held at Hippo (393) and Carthage (397) recognized a twenty-seven-book NT canon. Unanimity in the Western church was not fully achieved, but the twenty-seven-book canon was predominant. In the east, the Syrian church achieved a twenty-two-book canon by the fifth century, although later Christological controversies created division, resulting in some erosion of the fifth-century consensus.

Introduction of the Hebrew Scriptures: The inquiry of which *books* were to be considered canonical characterizes only the later stages of the configuration of the canonical anthologies. The oral and literary process used in the formation of the biblical literature took more than a thousand years, according to the best estimates of biblical research.

Scholars have argued that the Pentateuch is the final product of the interweaving of several literary sources, referred to as J, E, D, and P. The Yahwist source (J) is generally considered to be the earliest, dating from the period of the early monarchy (ca. 1000 B.C.). It is a narrative source that contains tales of the patriarchs, the Exodus, Sinai, and wilderness wanderings. Its most distinctive characteristic is its use of the divine name Yahweh (or Jahweh), from which comes the designation J or Yahwist. The Elohist source (E), which is characterized by its use of Elohim for the divine name prior to the theophany at the burning bush (Exod.

22

3), is a narrative fiber in many respects quite similar to J. Its portrayal of God is less anthropomorphic than that of J however, and it betrays special theological concerns, such as an interest in prophecy and a belief that the name Yahweh was first known when revealed to Moses at the burning bush. Scholars generally date E about a century later than J. The Deuteronomic source (D), dating from the period of the late monarchy (ca. seventh century B.C.), is confined largely to the book of Deuteronomy. Its concerns lie chiefly in its radical opposition to the worship of Baal; indeed, its program of restricting sacrifice to the Jerusalem Temple was developed for the purpose of stamping out Baal worship by outlawing sacrifice anywhere but Jerusalem. The Priestly source (P), dating from the period of the Babylonian exile (late sixth to early fourth centuries B.C.), emphasizes the cultic institutions of Israel: the Sabbath, circumcision, the role of Aaron (and, by implication, his priestly line), and the detailed legislation about cultic matters reportedly received at Sinai.

Attached to Deuteronomy was a Deuteronomistic edition of Joshua, Judges, Samuel, and Kings. This narrative of Israelite experience from the conquest of the land to the Babylonian exile reflects the Baal polemic and the program of centralization of sacrifice characteristic of Deuteronomistic theologians.

By the early postexilic period (late sixth century B.C.), the first two parts of the Hebrew Bible, the Torah and the Prophets, were almost complete. The section of the canon called the Writings was not finally completed until the second century B.C. The books of the Apocrypha (so-called) were written during the first two centuries B.C. and the first century A.D.

Introduction of the Christian New Testament: The NT also underwent a complex history of development. The English word "gospel" is derived from the Anglo-Saxon word *godspell,* which can mean either "a story about God," or "a good story." The later meaning is in harmony with the Greek work translated "gospel," *euangellion*, which means "good news." In secular Greek, *euangellion* referred to a good report about an important event. The 4 Gospels are the good news about the most significant events in all of history-the life, sacrificial death, and resurrection of Jesus of Nazareth.

When it comes to the composition of the Gospels, scholars generally agree that much of the material in the synoptic Gospels (Matthew, Mark, and Luke) originated in oral traditions, only later finding its way into written Gospels. Most scholars believe that Mark was the first of the Gospels to be written. The compilers of Matthew and Luke used Mark as a source. It is widely accepted that John is the latest of the four Gospels, though early traditions

24

may be contained within it. The synoptic Gospels were probably written between A.D. 70 and 100, with John coming in the late first or early second century.

The Letters of Paul were probably written in the 50s and 60s. Most of his writings erase any question to the authorship because his name is mentioned in the opening salutation; however, some have been under scrutiny. The catholic or general epistles (James, 1 and 2 Peter, Jude, 1, 2, and 3 John) probably emerged in the late first and early second centuries. It is likely that Hebrews and Revelation stem from the late first century.

Because of the aforementioned attributes, the presenter of the Word of God must guard against every mean and method of presenting the untruth of the Word. Truthful teaching and precisely preaching is a mandate from the Master and this mandate must be carried out.

Chapter Two

The Preparation of the Presenter

"Prepared through Prayer"

The messenger should remember that God is the foundation of the message therefore it is imperative that the presenter resides in close and continuous communion with Him. Prayer should be a holy habit that cannot be broken. It should be a mental exercise that keeps the head and heart of the messenger in shape for the leading of the Spirit as he works on the text. Prayer is what prompts and nurtures obedience, putting the heart into the proper "frame of mind" to desire obedience. It is important.

The essence of prayer is simply talking to God as you would to a beloved friend. The enemy would like nothing more than to keep the student of the Word from continuous communion with God. "Every generation faces the necessity to reprioritize and purify a corrupted or confused perception of prayer. For many, prayer has been replaced with pragmatic action. Function overrides fellowship with God; busyness crowds out communication. For others, prayer lacks a sense of awe and respect. Their efforts are flippant, disrespectful, and irreverent. Then there are those who believe prayer is designed to make demands and claims on God. They attempt to force Him to do what they believe He should do for them. Finally, for some prayer is nothing more than a routine ritual." [7]

Of course, knowledge is also important because it is necessary in understanding what God requires. However, knowledge and truth will remain abstract unless we commune with God in prayer. Prayer has a vital place in the life of the student of the Scripture. "First, it is an absolute prerequisite for salvation. Some people cannot hear; yet though deaf, they can be saved. Some may not be able to see; yet though blind, they can be saved. Knowledge of the Good News—salvation through the atoning death and resurrection of Jesus Christ—will come from one source or another, but in the final analysis, a person must humbly ask God for salvation. The prayer of salvation is the one prayer of the wicked God has said he will hear." [8]

Spurgeon states concerning the prayer life of the message giver, "It may scarcely be needful to commend to you the sweet

---

[7] MacArthur, J. 1995. *Alone with God.* Includes indexes. Victor Books: Wheaton, Ill.
[8] Sproul, R. 1996, c1991. *Following Christ.* Tyndale House Publishers: Wheaton, IL

uses of private devotion, and yet I cannot forbear. To you, as the ambassadors of God, the mercy-seat has a virtue beyond all estimates; the more familiar you are with the court of heaven the better shall you discharge your heavenly trust. Among all the formative influences which go to make up a man honored of God in the ministry, I know of none more mightily than his own familiarity with the mercy-seat. All that a college course can do for a student is coarse and external compared with the spiritual and delicate refinement obtained by communion with God." [9]   I have personally discovered that spending time on your knees at the foot of the Author of the Book will yield a greater harvest than commentaries, lexicons, or other study resources. The presenter must pray.

Why pray? Prayer, like everything else that is done by God's servants is for God's glory and for our benefit, in that order. "Everything that God does, everything that God allows and ordains, is in the supreme sense for his glory. It is also true that while God seeks his own glory supremely, man benefits when God is glorified. We pray to glorify God, but we also pray to receive the benefits of prayer from His hand. Prayer is for our benefit, even in light of the fact that God knows the end from the beginning. It is

---

[9] H. Spurgeon, *Lectures to My Students: Third Series* (reprint, Grand Rapids: Baker, 1977), 2

our privilege to bring the whole of our finite existence into the glory of his infinite presence."[10]

The preacher/teacher is called to a lifestyle of prayer, but many have come to see prayer as nothing more than an opportunity to call upon their Heavenly Butler for daily service, or cry out to their Heavenly Lifeguard when they are drowning in their daily circumstances. Certainly God has more for us than that. Jesus said that because He was going to the Father, we would do even greater works than He did (see John 14:12).

Prayer is the responsibility of the preacher/teacher because God's Word tells him to pray. He should not just pray because he has to; he prays because talking to God is a privilege. Prayer is entering into relationship with God so we can determine His will in the matter and call His will into existence upon the earth.

Prayer was the priority in Jesus' life. He considered it more important than *physical fitness*, and He was commonly pictured praying all night (see Luke 6:12). Talking with the Father took priority over *physical fellowship*. Scripture often refers to Jesus going off alone to be with the Father (see Matthew 14:23; Mark 1:35; Luke 5:16; Luke 6:12). And, finally, Jesus made prayer a priority over *physical food*. He fasted for long periods of time,

---

[10] Sproul, R. 1996, c1991. *Following Christ*. Tyndale House Publishers: Wheaton, IL

withdrawing from physical food to release spiritual power (see Luke 4:2; Matthew 6:18, 25, 31; Hebrews 7:25).

Prayer was the primary communication link between Himself and the Father. Every major event and every minor decision in Jesus' life was shrouded with prayer. If the expositor is going to be successful in his ministry, then he must follow Christ's example. Jesus did not pray because He had to; Jesus prayed because He wanted to remain in fellowship the Father. The presenter of the Word should desire the same fellowship. Prayer should be his priority.

There is an old cliché that speaks that seven days without prayer will make one weak. Prayer is the key to unlocking the power of God in the life of the presenter so he can effectively perform the ministry entrusted in his care by the Father. It does the presenter well to note that ministry to God must come before ministry to people.

The role of the priest is to minister first to God, then to the people. The way that we minister to God is by praising, worshiping and communing with Him through prayer. The way that we minister to the people is by allowing the overflow of what we have received in our time alone with God through prayer to pour out into the lives of others.

What role has prayer played during Bible times and since in the lives of the messengers of God? Let's review the following:

R. Kent Hughes, current senior pastor of the College Church of Wheaton, Illinois, assessed scores of books on preaching, and was frequently disappointed that authors said little or nothing about prayer. This led him to comment, "This, and what experience God so far has given me in preaching and prayer, has brought a conviction. Should I ever write a book on essentials for preaching, I know now that I would devote at least a *third* of it to spiritual preparation in matters such as prayer. This would be the *first* third."[11]

Bounds wrote, "The young preacher has been taught to lay out all his strength on the form, taste, and beauty of his sermon as a mechanical and intellectual product. We have thereby cultivated a vicious taste among the people and raised the clamor for talent instead of grace, eloquence instead of piety, rhetoric instead of revelation, reputation and brilliancy instead of holiness."[12]

---

[11] R. Kent Hughes, personal conversation, 21 December 1990; compare with Kent and Barbara Hughes, *Liberating Ministers from the Success Syndrome* (Wheaton, Ill.: Tyndale, 1987). The chapter "Success Is Prayer," pages 71–81, especially page 77, emphasizes the primacy of prayer; also cf. R. Kent Hughes, *Ephesians, The Mystery of the Body of Christ* (Wheaton, Ill.: Crossway, 1990), where he discusses Eph. 6:18–20.
[12] E. M. Bounds, *Power Through Prayer* (Grand Rapids: Baker, n.d.), 74.

Skill and supplication is the answer. The presenter of the Word must have a heavy prayer life. Bounds also wrote, "Light praying will make light preaching. Prayer makes preaching strong [the God who answers prayer does this] … and makes it stick." [13]

David Larsen, professor of homiletics at Trinity Evangelical Divinity School, also has emphasized prayer: "Strange it is that any discussion of preaching should take place outside the context of believing prayer. We have not prepared until we have prayed.…We cannot represent God if we have not stood before God. It is more important for me therefore to teach a student to pray than to preach.… " [14]

At an ordination of a man preparing to preach, Whyte advised, "Be up earlier than usual to meditate and pray over it. Steep every sentence of it in the Spirit. And pray after it." [15] The principle is that prayer should be the first priority in the life of the presenter. One cannot expect to make it to second base without a pit stop at first base. Prayer is that first base. Even after he circles all bases and hits home plate, prayer is needed.

---

[13] Ibid. 31.
[14] David Larsen, *The Anatomy of Preaching. Identifying the Issues in Preaching Today* (Grand Rapids: Baker, 1989), 53–54. Chapter 4 is helpful on spiritual preparation, stressing identity in Christ, the Word, prayer, the Spirit's power, and personal holiness.
[15] G. F. Barbour, *The Life of Alexander Whyte* (New York: George H. Doran, 1923), 296–97.

A famous Methodist preacher of England, William Sangster (1900–1960), felt closeness to God to be of utmost importance in preparing a message, "because after prayerful study, the preacher seems to fade out and leave the hearers face to face with God... If we are driven to make comparisons, we must insist that grace-gifts are more important than natural gifts. It is true that the Holy Spirit can work on very little, and if *effectiveness* is borne in mind rather than popularity, the unction of the Spirit is the greatest gift of all." [16]

For more than forty-six years George W. Truett (1867–1944) pastored the First Baptist Church in Dallas, Texas. After time with his family each evening, he went to his library to study and pray from 7 P.M. until midnight. [17] He also prepared at other hours. Once he was aboard a ship tossed by heavy winds and waves. The distress prompted a request for Truett to preach. He went alone with God, seeking a fitting message. After prayer, he found the message in Hebrews, "Ye have need of patience." When he announced his subject, the storm-weary people smiled their approval. [18]

---

[16] William Sangster, *The Approach to Preaching* (London: Epworth, 1951), 18; cf. also note 10 earlier in this chapter.
[17] Joe W. Burton, *Prince of the Pulpit* (Grand Rapids: Zondervan, 1946), 26.
[18] Ibid., 27.

34

The presenter as he prays should also pray for the message and the audience that will receive the message before and after he leaves the proclamation platform. This will succor in the presentation of the passage with the lips of the presenter and the patterning of the passage in the lives of the recipients with purity, passion, and power. The presenter needs to understand that sincere and serious prayer is necessary in order to successfully rightly divide the Word of truth. His living and his labor must be saturated with persisting and powerful praying. Prayer becomes the enforcer that keeps the focus on God and not on self.

The Word of God is a record of prayer — of praying men and their achievements. The success of the presenter cannot be experienced and enjoyed without being committed to prayer. Praying men have been God's vicegerent and voice on earth and only those men are used by God.

God's house is called "the house of prayer" because prayer is the most important of its holy offices; so by the same token, the Bible may be called the Book of Prayer. Prayer is the great theme and thesis of its message to mankind and it should be the great thought and task of the messenger. It is through the process and practice of prayer that the Word of God becomes open and operative to the preacher/teacher. The presenter who shares in the

35

"house of prayer" must have a "heart of prayer." There is power in prayer.

John Hyde prayed for speakers at conferences in India. He and R. M'Cheyne Paterson prayed for a month for a conference in 1904. George Turner joined them for three of those weeks. God saved hundreds of people and renewed believers. Hyde knelt for hours in his room or was prostrate on the floor, or he sat in on a message while interceding for the speaker and the hearers.

Dwight L. Moody (1837–1899), founder of the Moody Bible Institute, often saw God work in power when others prayed for his meetings in America and abroad. He often wired R. A. Torrey at the school, urging prayer. Faculty and students prayed all evening or into the early morning or all night.

After Moody's death, Torrey (1856–1928) preached in many countries. He, too, had prayer backing. In Australia, twenty-one hundred home prayer groups met for two weeks before he arrived; God turned many lives around. After Torrey died, Mrs. Torrey said, "My husband was a man of much prayer and Bible study. He denied himself social intercourse with even his best friends, in order that he might have time for prayer, study, and the preparation for his work." [19]

Torrey said to church members, "Pray for great things, expect great things, work for great things, but above all pray. Do you want a new minister? I can tell you how to get one. Pray for the one you have till God makes him over."[20] Torrey lived as if he believed prayer was the key that unlocks all the storehouses of God's infinite grace and power. He was for many years pastor of the Chicago Avenue Church in Chicago, Illinois, later called Moody Memorial Church. Much of the growth there resulted from prayer by Torrey and his praying people who met on Saturday nights and Sunday mornings.

These great leaders prayed diligently because they realized a very important fact in their ministries. They had an enemy who didn't want them to successfully deliver the Word of God. Ephesians tells us that our struggle is not against flesh and blood, but against the rulers, against the powers, against the world forces of this darkness, against the spiritual forces of wickedness in the heavenly places (Ephesians. 6:12). This is a call to do spiritual warfare through prayer over Satan's strongholds. Satan will usually attack in the area of our greatest strength because this is the

---

[19] R. A. Torrey, *The Power of Prayer and the Prayer of Power* (New York: Revell, 1924), 35.
[20] Ibid., 166

area in which we tend to rely on self and often find ourselves burning out from fighting our battles alone. Every area of your life is subject to enemy attack, so you must fight on your knees before you can stand on your mission field.

Jesus Himself had to battle Satan through prayer for His ministry and in other situations. We find this clearly illustrated in His wilderness temptation. He experienced spiritual warfare and won before He ever went out into public ministry.

Daniel's spiritual battle clearly illustrates the war that occurs in the heavenly realm of which the presenter of the Word must consciously be aware. "Then he said to me, fear not, Daniel: for from the first day that thou didst set your heart on understanding and to chasten thyself before your God, your words were heard, and I have come for thy words. But the prince of the kingdom of Persia withstood me for one and twenty days; but lo, Michael, one of the chief princes, came to help me, and I remained there with the kings of Persia" [21] (Daniel 10:12, 13).

Daniel's story exposes hold the enemy will try to hold up the prayers of those who seek the face of God for help to advance the agenda of God. Regardless of how he tries, he is fighting a losing battle.

---

[21] The King James Bible

Prayer should be considered as a great tool for the presenter and is paramount in balancing the dependency on human skills and the Holy Spirit. Both are needed to effectively and efficiently present the purity of the passage.

"Prepared Through Purity"

Happiness, not holiness, is the chief pursuit of most people today, including the preacher/teacher. People want Jesus to be their burden bearer and heavy load sharer but they desire to live like the devil. Purity in the form of holiness is a requirement for all who seek to represent God, especially those who are carriers of His Word. Personal holiness, being like Jesus- is the most important pursuit in the world.

The presenter of the Word of God must also be willing to present his mind and body to the Lord as a holy instrument or vessel to be used by God to bring glory to God. Each message should originate in the fertile heart of the preacher/teacher. If the presenter's heart is empty, his message will be empty; if the presenter's heart is full, his message will be full. Therefore, the presenter should keep his heart pure, and he should be filled with God's Word (Romans 12:1-2). The Word clearly declares that it is from the abundance of the heart that the mouth speaks.

Before the message is prepared, the presenter must be prepared; the presenter should first be prepared in his soul. Honest and holy preaching and teaching can only come if the presenter is saved. How can he have a message from God for the people of God without a personal relationship with God? Rarely one hears of the salvation of a preacher/teacher who has ministered for many years. This is, indeed, difficult to comprehend.

In addition to the messenger being prepared by purifying his soul, he must be prepared by purifying his mind. God uses all kinds of men to preach and teach to all kinds of people. Although this is the case, the presenter must remember that God never bestows a premium or payment on ignorance. He should have a desire to know, coupled with a careful discernment for truth. In addition to spending much time in the Scriptures, the preacher/teacher needs to have a system for developing his general knowledge.

It is also crucial that there be purity of the body. A preacher/teacher also needs to be prepared in his body. Care should be taken that the presenter does not abuse or neglect his body. It is not smart to say, "I'd rather burn out than rust out." Why do either? Jesus demonstrated the importance of taking care of the body when He told the disciples to come aside and rest awhile. Just as one would prepare himself mentally and spiritually, he should also prepare himself physically for the task of studying and proclaiming the Word.

Aside from the obvious mandate the Bible gives to moral purity in sexual, financial, and relational matters, the presenter who wants to cultivate a heart of integrity must strive to be triumphant over all the temptations of life that will seek to defile and destroy him and his ministry. "The Apostle Paul in his letter to young Timothy, his son in the ministry, gives him a command to "flee from these things" in 1 Timothy 6:10, 11. "Flee" is from the Greek word *pheugō*, from which the English word *fugitive* is derived. It is used in extra biblical Greek literature to speak of running from a wild animal, a poisonous snake, a deadly plague, or an attacking enemy. It is an imperative in the present tense and could be translated "keep on continually fleeing." A man of God is a lifelong fugitive, fleeing those things that would destroy him and his ministry. In other places Paul lists some of the threats: immorality (1 Cor. 6:18), idolatry (1 Cor. 10:14), false teaching (1 Tim. 6:20 and 2 Tim. 2:16), and false teachers (2 Tim. 3:5), as well as youthful lusts (2 Tim. 2:22).

A man of God must flee the evils associated with the love of money: various temptations, snares, harmful desires which lead to destruction, apostasy, and sorrow. Greed is the enemy. It will destroy the man of God, so he must run from it.

Love of money and material possessions is a characteristic sin of false teachers. From Balaam, that greedy prophet for hire (Deut. 23:4 and 2 Pet. 2:15), to Judas, who betrayed our Lord for thirty pieces of silver (Matt. 27:3); from the false prophets characterized by Isaiah as greedy dogs (Isa. 56:11) to the covetous prophets of Jeremiah's day (Jer. 6:13 and 8:10) and the prophets who prophesied for money, of whom Micah speaks (Mic. 3:11); from those slaves of their own appetites who deceived the Romans (Rom. 16:18) and the empty talkers and deceivers of Crete who upset whole families for the sake of sordid gain (Titus 1:11), all the way to the money-hungry televangelists and prosperity gospel preachers of our own day; false teachers have been characterized by greed.

But that is not true of a man of God. A man of God is not like those who, in Paul's words, are "peddling the word of God" (2 Cor. 2:17). He is not a spiritual con artist. He has to proclaim God's message, not what he thinks will sell. He is in the business of piercing men's hearts with God's truth, not tickling their ears. He does nothing for personal gain."[22]

Although the presenter is to flee from the things that will destroy his ministry, he is also commanded to follow after the

---

[22] MacArthur, J. 1997, c1992. *Rediscovering Expository Preaching*. Word Pub.: Dallas, p.86-87

42

things that will develop his ministry. In the second part of 1 Tim. 6:11, Paul lists six virtues every man of God should follow after: righteousness, godliness, faith, love, perseverance, and gentleness. The word "follow" (dioôke) is strong word meaning to run after; to run swiftly after; to hotly pursue; to seek eagerly and earnestly. It has the idea of aiming at and pursuing until something is gained; of never giving up until we have reached our goal.

"Righteousness" (in Greek, *dikaiosunē*) means being right with God. It is having a heart that is right with God through the Lord Jesus Christ. It refers to the right behavior toward both God and man. The reference here is not to imputed righteousness received at salvation, but to the practical righteousness to be exhibited in our lives because of the divine nature of God in our hearts.

"Godliness" (in Greek, *eusebeia*) is closely connected with righteousness. Righteousness may speak of outward conduct, godliness of the inward attitude. Godliness means to live in the reverence and awe of God; to be so conscious of God's presence that one lives just as God would live if He were walking upon earth. It means to live seeking to be like God; to seek to possess the very character, nature, and behavior of God. The man of God follows and runs after godliness. He seeks to gain a consciousness of God's presence—a consciousness so intense that he actually

43

lives as God would live if He were on earth. It is the spirit of holiness, reverence, and piety that directs righteous behavior. Right behavior flows from a right attitude; correct conduct flows from proper motive. The basic meaning of *eusebeia* is reverence for God. The man characterized by *eusebeia* has a worshiping heart. He knows what it means to "live in the fear of thc LORD always" (Prov. 23:17). He not only does right, but also thinks right; he not only behaves properly, but also is properly motivated. He is a man who serves God with reverence and awe (Heb. 12:28). Though he lives his life in the conscious presence of the holiness of God, paradoxically he may feel very unholy, like Isaiah (cf. Isaiah 6).

"Faith" (in Greek, *pistis*) means both to believe and to be faithful. The man of God seeks faith: to learn to trust God more and more; to be a man of faith, a man of great faith and belief. He wants to believe, trust, and depend upon God—to grow more and more in believing God. He wants to be loyal, obedient, and attached to God. He wants to please God in all that he does. He places his trust in God for everything, an absolute loyalty to the Lord. It is unwavering confidence in God's power, plan, provision, protection, presence, and promise. The man of God lives by faith. He trusts in the sovereign God to keep His word, to meet all his needs, and provide the resources he needs to pursue his ministry.

"Love" (in Greek, *agapē*) refers to a volitional love, not an emotional feeling. It is a love that is unrestricted, unrestrained, and unconditional. It should be interpreted in this passage in its broadest sense. It means love to everybody—love to God, men, believers, and non-believers.

"Perseverance" (in Greek, *hupomonē*) means to be steadfast, to endure, and to persevere. The word literally means "to remain under." It is not passive resignation, but victorious, triumphant endurance, an unswerving loyalty to the Lord in the midst of trials.

"Gentleness" (in Greek, *praupathia*) is the second external virtue. It can also be translated "meekness" or "humility." Gentleness has a strong state of mind. It looks at situations and wants justice and right to be done. It is not a weak mind that ignores and neglects evil and wrong-doing, abuse and suffering. The man of God has nothing to boast about. Paul he recognizes that though he labors, it is God's power working through him that brings effectiveness in ministry (cf. Col. 1:29). The man of God has the mind of Christ—the mind of humility (Phil. 2:18).

Purity was required of God for those who would work in His house. Just as it was required then, it is required now. We must remember that the Holy Word of God should be handled with holy hands and a holy heart. A study of the Jewish priesthood reveals that God insisted that the priests be holy men, pure in their person and purpose, set apart for His service alone. The presenter must pattern his lifestyle in such a way that he is set aside for the service of serving the Word of God. The following are quarters of preparation that qualify the presenter to proclaim the Word:

- The preacher/teacher must be a truly regenerated believer in Jesus Christ. He must be a part of God's redeemed family (John 1:12–13). If a man is to deliver a personal message from the heavenly Father effectively, he must be a legitimate spiritual son or the message will inevitably be distorted.
- The preacher/teacher must be appointed and gifted by God to the teaching/preaching ministry (Eph. 4:11–16 and 1 Tim. 3:2). Unless a man is divinely enabled to proclaim, he will be inadequate, possessing only human ability.
- The preacher/teacher must be inclined and trained to be a student of God's Word. Otherwise, he cannot carry out the mandate of 2 Tim. 2:15 to "cut straight" the Word of God's truth.

- The preacher/teacher must be a mature believer who demonstrates a consistent godly character (1 Tim. 3:2–3).
- The preacher/teacher must be dependent upon God the Holy Spirit for divine insight and understanding of God's Word (1 Cor. 2:14–15). Without the Spirit's illumination and power, the message will be relatively impotent.
- The preacher/teacher must be in constant prayerful communion with God to receive the full impact of the Word (Ps. 119:18). The obvious one to consult for clarification is the original author.
- The preacher/teacher must first let the developing message sift through his own thinking and life before he can preach/teach it. Ezra provides the perfect model in that he set his heart to study the law of God and to practice it, and to teach God's statues and ordinances in Israel (Ezra 7:10).

A comprehensive study of the Book of Leviticus will also expose five basic themes that relate to the important of a life of holiness: a *holy God*; a *holy minister*; a *holy multitude*; a *holy ground*; and a *holy Messiah*.

The Hebrew word for "holy" that Moses used in Leviticus means "that which is set apart and marked off, that which is different." The Sabbath was holy because God set it apart for His people (Ex. 16:23). The priests were holy because they were set apart to minister to the Lord (Lev. 21:7–8). Their garments were holy and could not be duplicated for common use (Ex. 28:2). The tithe that the people brought was holy (Lev. 27:30). Anything that God said was holy had to be treated differently from the common things of life in the Hebrew camp. In fact, the camp of Israel was holy, because the Lord dwelt there with His people (Deut. 23:14).

Our English word "holy" comes from the Old English word *halig* which means "to be whole, to be healthy." What health is to the body, holiness is to the inner person. The related word "sanctify" comes from the Latin *sanctus* which means "consecrated, sacred, blameless." We use the word "sanctification" to describe the process of growing to become more like Christ, and "holy" to describe the product of being grown like Christ.

Because of the immorality and idolatry of the Canaanites and the future mythological deities of the Greek and the Romans, God mandated His followers to avoid this type of behavior because He was a holy God. As *holy Master*, He revealed His holiness in the following ways:

To begin with, He gave them *a holy commandment* while on Mt. Sinai that contained both precious promises and punishing penalties know as the Ten Commandments (Ex. 20:1–17). These commandments informed the people of what was right and wrong in the eye of God and served as daily guidelines for daily going. The consequences for disobedience were also relayed.

At Mt. Sinai, God also revealed His *holy company.* He revealed His holiness through the thunderings, and the lightnings, and the noise of the trumpet, and the mountain smoking (20:18; see 19:14–25). The people hid themselves from the holiness of His presence.

The *holy comos* (power) of God was also manifested during the judgment of the gods of Egypt when He opened the Red Sea and destroyed the Egyptian army (14:13–15:21), and when He did miraculous works for Israel in the wilderness.

His holiness is also seen in His *holy castle.* God, who is full of holiness, is found dwelling in the holy of holies in both the tabernacle (40:34–38) and the temple (1 Kings 8:10). The presence of the cloud of glory during the day and the pillar of fire at night served as a reminder to Israel of the holiness of God. He was referred to as a "consuming fire" (Deut. 4:24; Heb. 12:29). A study of the structure of the tabernacle of God even declares the holiness of God: the fence around the tent, the brazen altar where the blood was shed, and the laver where the priests washed their hands and feet, and the veil that kept everybody but the high priest out of the holy of holies. In declaration and demonstration, God made it clear to the people of Israel that He is a holy God, righteous in all His works and just in all His judgments.

The *holy minister* is a representative of the holiness of God. The Jewish priesthood belonged only to the tribe of Levi. Levi, the founder of the tribe, was the third son of Jacob and Leah (Gen. 29:34; 35:23) and the father of Gershom, Kohath, and Merari (46:11). Since Kohath's son Amram was the father of Aaron, Moses, and Miriam (Num. 26:58–59), Aaron, Moses, and Miriam belonged to the tribe of Levi.

Aaron was the first high priest and his male descendants became priests, with the firstborn son in each generation inheriting the high priesthood. (Every priest was a Levite, but not every Levite was a priest.) The rest of the men in the tribe of Levi (the "Levites") were assigned to serve as assistants to the priests. They served in the role of assistant ministers. The Levites were the substitutes for the firstborn males in Israel, all of whom had to be dedicated to the Lord (Ex. 13:1–16; Num. 3:12–13, 44–51). To smooth the progress of their ministry, David eventually divided the thousands of Levites into twenty-four "courses" (1 Chron. 23:6). The name "Leviticus" comes from "Levi" and means "pertaining to the Levites." God required these men to be holy ministers, set apart for His service alone.

God required them to be separated from many things to preserve their holiness. One requirement was that they come from the tribe of Levi, but also they must not have any physical defects or marry women of whom God disapproved (chaps. 21–22). They were set apart in an elaborate ceremony that involved their being bathed in water and marked by oil and blood (chap. 8). The high priest was anointed with special oil. The priests wore special garments, and special laws that didn't apply to the common people governed their lives. In every way, the priests demonstrated the fact that they were set apart and therefore holy to the Lord.

These holy ministers were responsible for caring for the sanctuary of God. As Israel traveled through the wilderness they were responsible for carrying the tent and its furnishings from place to place (Num. 1:47–54). They were also responsible for guarding God's sanctuary (1 Chron. 9:19), to teach the people the Law (Deut. 33:8–11; Neh. 8:7–9), and for lead the worshipers in praising God (1 Chron. 9:28–32).

Cleanliness was also a requirement. Those that served God in the temple had to be dressed properly. If the priests weren't dressed properly (Ex. 28:39–43), if they didn't wash properly (30:20–21), or if they tried to serve while unclean (Lev. 22:9), they were in danger of death. If the Levites were careless with the tabernacle furnishings, they too might die (Num. 4:15, 20). The high priest wore a golden plate at the front of his turban on which was the inscription, "Holiness to the Lord" (Ex. 28:36); and he dared not do anything that would violate that inscription. He could be serving in the holy of holies in the tabernacle and still be in danger of death (Lev. 16:3).

Israel begins what I call the *holy multitude*. God's purpose for Israel was that the nation be a holy nation (Ex. 19:6). Everything in the life of the Old Testament Jew was either "holy" (set apart for God's exclusive use) or "common," and the "common" things were either "clean" (the people could use them) or "unclean" (it was forbidden to use them). The Jews had to be careful to avoid what was unclean; otherwise, they would find themselves "cut off from the people" until they had gone through the proper ceremony to be made clean again.

God's laws governing marriage, birth, diets, personal cleanliness, the quarantine of diseased persons, and the burial of the dead-while they certainly involved hygienic benefits to the nation-were all reminders that God's people couldn't live any way they pleased because they were God's chosen people and had been called to a life of holiness. (Lev. 10:10). They were challenged and commanded not to live like the godless nations around them.

The *holy multitude* is composed of those who are true followers of Jesus Christ who are referred to as priest of God (1 Peter 2:5, 9). God reveals His holiness through these believers. In the Old Testament, God's people had a *representative* priesthood; but in the New Testament, God's people are *representatives* of the priesthood (Rev. 1:6). Through faith in Christ, we've been washed (1 Cor. 6:9–11), clothed in His righteousness (2 Cor. 5:21), anointed by the Spirit (1 John 2:20, 27) and given access into His presence (Heb. 10:19–20).

The Body of Christ, the church, is supposed to be "a holy nation" in this present evil world. As a holy nation, the church should declare the praises of God who called her out of darkness into His wonderful light (1 Peter 2:9). The Greek word translated "declare" means "to tell out, to advertise." The holy nation of Israel in Canaan, with its holy priesthood, revealed to the pagan nations around them the praises and power of God. The church in today's world has the same privilege and responsibility. The holiness of God should be revealed through His followers.

What is the *holy ground*? This is a reference to the holy land of God. Not only do the people belong to God, but also the property. A holy God wants His holy people to live in a holy land.

In Leviticus 18–27, the word "land" is used sixty-eight times. In these chapters, Moses named the sins that defile the land

and invite divine judgment: immorality (chap. 18); idolatry (chap. 19); capital crimes (chap. 20); blasphemy (chap. 23); and refusing to give the land its rest (chap. 25). Unfortunately, the Jewish people committed all these sins and more; God had to chasten them by allowing Babylon to destroy Jerusalem and take the people captive (2 Chron. 36:14–21).

The nations of the world today don't have the same covenant relationship to God that Israel has, but they are still responsible to obey His moral law and use His gifts wisely (Amos 1–2). I can't speak about other nations, but I believe my own beloved land is guilty of abusing God's gifts and refusing to obey God's laws, and is therefore ripe for judgment. The very sins that God condemns—murder, deceit, immorality, violence, greed, and blasphemy—are the very things that entertain the masses, whether it's on television or in movies or books. Take the violence and vice out of entertainment and many people won't pay to see it.

God even gave His people an annual calendar to follow to help them appreciate His gifts and use them for His glory (chaps. 23, 25). Until after the Babylonian Captivity, the Jews were primarily an agricultural people; and the calendar of feasts was tied directly to the annual harvests. The Sabbatical Years and the Year of Jubilee not only helped conserve the land, they also helped regulate the economy of the nation. The ungodly nations could just look at the land of Israel and see that Jehovah was blessing His people and caring for them!

We have a *holy Messiah* who reveals the holiness of God. Why do we have a holy Messiah? No amount of good works or religious efforts can make a sinner holy. Only the blood of Jesus Christ can cleanse us from our sins (1 John 1:7), and only the risen glorified Savior can intercede for us at the throne of God as our Advocate (2:1) and high priest (Heb. 8:1 ; Rom. 8:34). The holiness of the Messiah is manifested in the cleansing power of the blood. The blood of the Lamb can transform a polluted soul to a purified soul.

God wants the believer to be a "holy priesthood" and a "holy nation" so that he will advertise His nature and glorify His name (1 Peter 2:5, 9). The reputation of God is concealed in His nature and name. When His people, through a lack of purity, live as an "unholy priesthood" and "unholy nation," it serves as an indictment against the holiness of God. Eight times in His Word, the Lord says, "Be holy, for I am holy!" The presenter of the Word must seek to present himself in the beauty of holiness.

"Prepared By Power"

It would be very beneficial to the presenter of the Word to understand the relationship and role of the Holy Spirit in the

55

preaching/teaching ministry. He serves as the co-laborer, the partner to the presenter. The presenter will discover that it is impossible to grasp an accurate and applicable understanding of God's intended revelation in Scripture without the ministry of the Holy Spirit. It is the Spirit of God that illuminates and instructs the student of the Scripture to the true meaning of the Master in the message. God desires, through the Spirit, to open the eyes of the messenger and give His revelation. The prophet Isaiah speaks of the Holy Spirit's role as Teacher. "And the spirit of the LORD shall rest upon him, the spirit of wisdom and understanding, the spirit of counsel and might, the spirit of knowledge and of the fear of the LORD" (Isa. 11:2)." [23] The wisdom and understanding of the passage imparted upon the presenter by the Holy Spirit empowers him to handle the Word with accuracy. What the presenter must seek to do is to yield himself to the tutorage of the Spirit and allow Him to manifest the truths of God which He can only reveal. "But God hath revealed *them* unto us by his Spirit: for the Spirit searcheth all things, yea, the deep things of God." (1 Cor. 2:10). [24]

The following passages also reveal that the Holy Spirit empowers the presenter for the preaching/teaching ministry:

---

[23] *The Holy Bible: King James Version. 1995. Logos Research Systems, Inc.: Oak Harbor, WA*
[24] *The Holy Bible: King James Version. 1995. Logos Research Systems, Inc.: Oak Harbor, WA*

- For to one is given by the Spirit the word of wisdom; to another the word of knowledge by the same Spirit (1 Cor. 12:10).

- Turn you at my reproof: behold, I will pour out my spirit unto you, I will make known my words unto you (Proverbs 1:23).

- For to one is given by the Spirit the word of wisdom; to another the word of knowledge by the same Spirit (1 Cor. 12:8).

"But the Comforter, which is the Holy Ghost, whom the Father will send in my name, he shall teach you all things, and bring all things to your remembrance, whatsoever I have said unto you (John 14:26)." [25] Illumination, though often considered secondary to revelation and inspiration, is equally important. Without revelation and inspiration, we would have no Bible. Without illumination, we can have no accurate understanding of the Bible. It would be of little use to have a special revelation from God that no one could understand. So illumination is the culmination of the revelatory process.

The need for illumination begins at the time of initial salvation. Unbelievers cannot properly understand Scripture

---

[25] *The Holy Bible: King James Version. 1995. Logos Research Systems, Inc.: Oak Harbor, WA*

because the Gospel is veiled to them and they are blinded by Satan (2 Cor. 4:3–4). "That veil must be supernaturally lifted (2 Cor. 3:16). Since fallen man is dead to the things of God (Eph. 2:1), the Spirit must remove his limitation and impart an understanding of saving spiritual truth." [26]

Scripture teaches that there must be a relationship with the Author of the Book before one can apply spiritual truths to his life. This is vocalized in 1 Corinthians 2:11–12, where Paul explains that the Spirit of God communicates with the spirit of the child of God, the one who possesses His Spirit, to teach him those things that can be understood in no other way. Others can certainly comprehend facts about the Bible and see important biblical principles for life. But the veil imposed by sin prevents a person from taking the Bible and relating it successfully to life without the specific ministry of the third Person of the Godhead, the divine Author of Scripture. Furthermore, the believer who is consistently controlled by the Spirit (Eph. 5:18) will be better able to appropriate God's revelation than one who is not, according to 1 Corinthians 2:13.

The Bible teaches in 2 Timothy 2:15 that the Word should be handled carefully. This principle teaches that nothing should

---

[26]Macarthur, J. 1997, c1992. *Rediscovering Expository Preaching*. Word Pub.: Dallas

58

just be assumed. Do not take anything for granted. Lay aside any preconceived notions. Do not be bound by tradition, because no system of doctrine, no matter how old or how highly respected, can ever be a substitute for the Word of God. At every point, the question every one of us must ask ourselves "For what saith the Scripture?" (Rom 4:3). Then we must be ready to do what it says. Be willing even to be startled by what we discover, and boldly put it into practice.

Remember the relationship and role of the Holy Spirit in the preaching/teaching ministry and trust Him for guidance into all truth. Jesus, during his preaching ministry declared his trust in the Spirit when He announced: *"The Spirit of the LORD is upon Me, Because He has anointed Me To preach the gospel to the poor; He has sent Me to heal the brokenhearted, To preach deliverance to the captives And recovery of sight to the blind, To set at liberty them that are bruised; To preach the acceptable year of the LORD* (LUKE 4:18, 19)." [27] It was through the power of the Spirit that He performed the work. Like Jesus, the presenter of the Word must lean and depend on the Spirit of God to perform the task of truthful teaching and precisely preaching.

---

[27] *The Holy Bible: King James Version. 1995. Logos Research Systems, Inc.: Oak Harbor, WA*

Chapter Three

The Processing of the Passage

"Reading the Passage"

Processing the passage begins with a saturation process. The saturation process involves reading and storing as much material as possible without taking very many notes. Once the preacher/teacher has assimilated and attached himself to the passage to be presented, he may then proceed to saturate his mind with that passage. The first and the foremost piece of material that should be used in the saturation process is the Bible. The student needs to diligently consume and digest as much of the Scripture relevant to his message as he can. He should chew on it over and over again by reading it from various translations. Once he has done this, he may then carefully study commentaries and any other resource material available.

In an endeavor to effectively express the earnestness of the passage the presenter must begin the development process of the biblical text. "A man cannot hope to preach the Word of God accurately until he has first engaged in a careful, exhaustive exegesis of his text. Herein lies the problem, for competent

61

exegesis requires time, brain power, "blood, sweat, and tears," all saturated with enormous doses of prayer."[28] This process begins with the careful reading of the text. The text should be read with an open and receptive mind in order for the Word to take root in the heart of the presenter. A closed mind is a mark of an unreceptive attitude which will cause the reader to poison the passage with personal impurities derived from the human flesh.

The presenter must become totally committed to reading the Word because there is no substitute for the reading of the Word of God. Other books may also be read during the study process, but nothing should take the place of the Word. I have found it helpful to read through the book that the passage is being taken from to get a good understanding of the period, people, practices, and principles being revealed. It is also helpful to take study notes as you read. Remember, there is no other way to know what the Bible has to say but to read it.

The following errors should be avoided in reading the Bible:

- Don't make the Bible say what you want it to say.
- Don't become superficial in your reading and start deriving your own conclusion on what the Bible is saying.

---

[28] John A. Sproule, "Biblical Exegesis and Expository Preaching" (unpublished lecture at Grace Theological Seminary, Winona Lake, Ind., 1978), 1.

- Don't spiritualize the Bible and turn it into a fairy tale story. Get the right meaning from the reading of the text.

The question is often asked, which version of the Bible should I read? There are many translations of the Bible available for the reader today. The Bible was originally written in three languages: Hebrew, Greek, and Aramaic. The King James Version is the best and closest translation to the original languages; therefore, it should be highly favored.

Once you have decided which version of the Bible you are going to read then the next step is to select the biblical text to be studied. There are many ways to do this. A good starting place is by picking a book of the Bible and start reading, beginning with the first verse of the first chapter. As you read, you may find you respond emotionally to something you read. You may be comforted, curious, confused, convicted, challenged, disturbed, angry, or moved emotionally. Select that emotionally stirring sentence, verse, or paragraph to study. Carefully and consciously read the selected Bible text to be studied. Focus on what the text actually says and write your observations. A famous author once wrote, "The pen is the crowbar of the mind." Writing your thoughts will stimulate more ideas.

French offers the following example in reading the text. "I began reading Philippians Chapter 1. As I read this chapter, I was amazed by Paul's response to those who preach the Gospel with bad motives in Philippians 1:18–19. So I decided to study Philippians 1:18–19, which reads: "What then? notwithstanding, every way, whether in pretense, or in truth, Christ is preached; and I therein do rejoice, Yea, and will rejoice. " So now I will list my observations as follows:

- Paul said that what mattered to him was that people preached about Christ. He rejoiced because people preached about Christ, regardless of their motives for telling others about Jesus and the Gospel.

- Taking Philippians 17 and 18 together, Paul rejoiced that people preached about Christ even though some of them preached about Christ in order to cause even more trouble for Paul. Paul was in plenty of trouble. He was in prison waiting for a trial to determine if he would be put to death for preaching about Christ (Philippians 1:7, 12–13, 16, 9–20). If that were not bad enough, Paul learned that some fellow believers were among those trying to make his troubles even worse. But Paul had an amazingly good attitude in such bad circumstances!

- How did Paul develop such a good attitude? According to Philippians 1:12–18, what mattered most to Paul was that people preached about Christ and that spread the Gospel. People preached about Christ much more because Paul was in prison for his faith. That caused him to rejoice regardless of their motives for telling others about Christ. Not only that, Paul continued to rejoice because he expected God to answer the believers' prayers so that everything, including the actions of his enemies, would result in his release from prison (Philippians 1:18–19). He also expected the Holy Spirit to help him (Philippians 1:19)." [29]

Macarthur adds, "The first step in studying an individual passage is to read it. I read it repeatedly in my Bible until it is pretty well fixed in my memory. I try to do that early in the week of preaching it or even before, so I have time to meditate on it. Before I get into actual preparation, I want to be mentally grappling with the passage. Once I begin concentrating on my sermon text, it dominates my thinking, conversation, and reading during my time of preparation. All this begins with becoming familiar with the text. I rarely consciously memorize Scripture, but by the time I finish preparing the sermon, I usually have the text pretty well memorized."[30]

The text should be read repeatedly until its theme, meaning the main truth of the passage, is understood. Reading for many

---

[29] French, R. A. 1999. *Diving for pearls in God's treasure chest: An easy way to study the Bible*. Logos Research Systems, Inc.: Oak Harbor, WA
[30] MacArthur, J. 1997, c1992. *Rediscovering expository preaching* . Word Pub.: Dallas

individuals may only be a hobby, but to the serious student and sharer of the Word it should be a holy habit that is unbreakable. This holy habit should be practiced over and over again.

"Researching the Passage"

The student of the Scripture will find that he must adopt several policing characteristics that are detective and exploratory in nature as he searches for the truth of the Word. "In searching out God's message, he is a "Columbus" navigating the expansive seas of Scripture to bring news of a fairer world. He is a "Sherlock Holmes" poking for clues that will cause God's truth, justice, and mercy to prevail. He is akin to Catton, who in his famous Civil War trilogy, delves into history and casts events in their original light." [31] The expositor digs for gold and drills for oil as he searches the Scriptures with diligence and determination.

This process of researching the passage is known as studying. The primary difference between reading and researching the Bible involves two additional activities: asking questions of the text and writing down your insight. Here are several principles of interpretation that will aid in presenting the purity of the passage.

---

[31] W. B. Catton, *Bruce Catton's Civil War* (New York: Fairfax, 1984).

MacArthur articulates the following on the researching process. "First, the relationship between using hermeneutics (rules of interpretation) and doing exegesis and exposition needs to be kept in mind:

1.   Use the true text, God's Word, as closely as you can responsibly determine it by consulting specialists on textual criticism.

2.   Employ the science of hermeneutics, with its interpretive principles.

3.   Let these principles expose the meaning of a passage (i.e., do an exegetical study of the text) as a person follows prescribed rules in playing a game. Exegesis, then, is the application of hermeneutical principles to decide what a text says and means in its own historical, theological, contextual, literary, and cultural setting. The meaning thus obtained will be in agreement with other related Scriptures.

4.   Preach the exposition that flows from this process. Make conspicuous the true and essential original meaning and apply this

meaning to present needs of hearers in their own cultural situation."[32]

These principles represent the historically recognized process of interpreting and proclaiming the Word. They will act as a safe guard from falling into the trap of imposing ones own claim on what the passage is actually saying and cause him to inform God's claim. The expositor is an investigator of the passage and not an imposer of the passage.

There are several terms that the student should become familiar with that will help him acquire the fullness from the researching process as he uses other sources of study material. These terms will help to further his understanding in the proclamation ministry.

Three Types of Proclamations:

- *Topical Proclamation:* the combining of a series of Bible verses that loosely connect with a theme.
- *Textual Proclamation:* the usage of a short text or passage that generally serves as a gateway into whatever subject the preacher chooses to address.

---

[32] John F. MacArthur, Jr., "The Mandate of Biblical Inerrancy: Expository Preaching," *The Master's Seminary Journal* 1, no. 1 (Spring 1990): 3–15, especially 9–10.

- *Expository Proclamation:* the predominant focus on the text(s) under consideration along with its context(s). *Terminology of Proclamations:*
- *Homiletics:* the rooting of the structure and the spirit for the message's delivery in the text.
- *Hermeneutics:* the science of the correct interpretation of the Bible.

Expository preaching/teaching can be summed up in three key words: *Inductive, Exegetical*, and *Expositional*.

- *Inductive*: approaching the text to find out what it means, letting it speak for itself.
- *Exegetical:* presenting the text after research and study has been completed.
- *Expositional:* approaching the Word of God *inductively*, studying it *exegetically*, and then explaining it to the people in an *expositional* manner.

Expository proclamation seeks to clarify what is difficult to understand in a passage. It opens up the Word to expose Its meaning. It is analogous to pulling back the curtains for the listener, facilitating the entry of light and the unclouding of one's spiritual eye.

There is a need for the student to *exercise commitment to the context*. Robert A. French had this to say about the context of the passage being researched, "It always helps to study a larger context than is required, but studying too small a context can lead to error. What is the *context?* The written *context* of any text is the larger body of material surrounding the text. For example:

- The context of a *word* is the *sentence* it appears in.
- The context of a *sentence* is the *paragraph* it appears in.
- The context of a *paragraph* is the *topic* it appears in.
- The context of a *topic* is the *section* it appears in.
- The context of a *section* is the *division* it appears in.
- The context of a *division* is the *book* it appears in.
- The context of a *book* is *all that author wrote* in the Bible.
- The context of *all that an author wrote* in the Bible is the *part of the Old or New Testament* his works appear in (e.g. historical books, poetic books, prophetic books, gospels, letters, etc.).
- The context of *part of the Old or New Testament* is the *entire Old or New Testament.*

- The context of the *Old or New Testament* is the *whole Bible*." [33]

The presenter should seek to study the passage in light of its context. To take a verse out of its setting and subscribe a false and foreign meaning is a dangerous and defiling presentation of the Holy Scriptures. The context principle is that principle by which God gives light upon a subject through either near or remote passages bearing upon the same theme. Every sentence or verse in the Bible has something that precedes it and something that follows it - except Genesis 1:1 and Revelation 22:21. The presenter should become an investigator and observe every clue regarding what a context says explicitly and also what it does not say. Like the television detective Monk, he should search and search for contextual evidence that will serve as biblical proof to be presented from the passage. The following clues should be carefully investigated in context:

- The significance of verb tenses and connecting words such as "and," "therefore," and "for."
- The series of participles (words having the characteristic of both verb and adjective) in a particular passage.

---

[33] French, R. A. 1999. *Keys to the Bible's treasures: How to determine the meaning of Bible texts.* Logos Research Systems, Inc.: Oak Harbor, WA

- The systematic repetition of a word(s) that pleas for the researcher's attention.
- The stated contrasts within the context.

As the preacher/teacher diligently seeks to find the treasury of truth from the text his primary focus should be the details of the context. These will serve as clues that will lead to more gold from the Gospel. That's why it is so important to dig, dig, and dig a context. The more digging, and the more drilling, the more oil from the Word is discovered. Let the student of the Word seek to strike it rich in the Scriptures.

There is also the need for the preacher/teacher to *explore the glamour of grammar*. Grammar is the study of the classes of words, their inflections, and their functions, in relation to the sentence. It is helpful to be sharpened and skilled in the fundamentals of grammar because it is used to elucidate and expose the mind of the writer's intent. Knowing the original language of the Bible will serve as a great advantage to the student of the Scriptures.

Regardless of whether the presenter has learned biblical grammar well in seminary, faithful study in good sources is beneficial. In either case, he can improve if he dedicates himself to learning grammar and using good tools. He can be enlightened and enriched by the writings of experts in sentence structures, exegetical commentaries, and journal pieces of writing. A good understanding of biblical grammar will eliminate the presenter's dependence on books written for popular appeal at the shallow level of a light, generalized Sunday school quarterly or lower. Why should he be limited to drinking from the wells of writers who have a knack for teaching error with a colorful flair? Why not zealously assure sound results in dependable works and then correlate what is learned with all the interpretive principles, including grammar? Prayer for God's guidance all along the way is necessary, because God, whose servant the expositor is, has the most concern that he get His message straight.

Along with *exercising commitment to context* and *exploring the glamour of the grammar, extensive working on words* that are chief and central within the passage will provide the presenter with precious and powerful possessions to be proclaimed. The expositor should focus on every word of the text but special attention should be allocated and applied to key words. A detailed study of the words of the text will also help in determining whether the usage is literal or figurative. A good practice to keep in mind for determining the literal or figurative application of the text is to always start with the literal idea and remain there unless it makes no sense.

One of the most valuable tools for assistance in understanding the Bible is a concordance. It is simply an index to words or phrases in the Bible. Its importance for study springs from the nature of the Bible as a unified book. Since scripture has one Author, the Holy Spirit, it must throughout be a result of uniform intentions. What is said in one portion is usually related to information somewhere else. Using a concordance gives assent to the principle that Scripture is its own best interpreter.

One could quickly find in a concordance, for example, that the living creatures in Ezekiel 1 are cherubs. They appear in chapter 10 and are connected with chapter 1 in 10:15 ff., and in 10:20 the explicit identification is made. But where else do cherubs appear in the Bible? An examination of a complete concordance would reveal that they are found in Strong's Concordance, for instance, in the following books (eighty-nine times altogether): Genesis, Exodus, Numbers, 1 and 2 Samuel, 1 and 2 Kings, 1 and 2 Chronicles, Psalm, Isaiah., and Ezekiel. Study of these passages will reveal that cherubs are seen in Scripture at points where the intimate presence of God is described: the Garden of Eden, the Ark of the Covenant, etc. Their mention in Ezekiel 1 contributes to this picture by delineating them as occupied in some way with the glory of God.

"A concordance lists all the passages where a word occurs. The sermon-maker can find in his Bible—Hebrew and Greek texts as well as English—the settings of a word in a given Bible book, writer, or in the Old Testament and New Testament. In a lexicon he locates possible meanings the word can have in differing situations. His task is to find the right idea in the setting of his present text.

For example, *lion* has several meanings in Scripture: an animal frightening in power, Babylon as a terrifying invader (Jer. 4:7), the nation Israel or a leader (Ezek. 19:2)," [34] an analogy for Satan (1 Pet. 5:8), and Christ (Rev. 5:5), to name several. Behind each are the ideas of awesome power, authority, and ability to overcome.

One can add colorful details by consulting a lexicon. Barber lists a number of lexicons in *The Minister's Library*. The more helpful Old Testament works are by Brown/Driver/Briggs, Holladay, and Koehler and Baumgartner. Valuable New Testament aid is available in Abbott-Smith and Arndt and Gingrich. Other profitable lexical works are the two-volume *Theological Wordbook of the Old Testament* by R. Laird Harris, et al. (Chicago: Moody,

---

[34] Howard, and N. Turner (1908–76), and A. T. Robertson (1934). For most purposes, preachers will find what they need in Weingreen, Dana/Mantey, and Robertson.

75

1980) and Vine's *Expository Dictionary* (cf. notes 8 and 10 in this chapter). The latter lists each word in English, then (in the edition cited, note 10) keys the Hebrew or Greek for each word to the numbering system in *Strong's Concordance.*

Other resources that convey the riches of biblical words include *The New Bible Dictionary,* edited by J. D. Douglas (Grand Rapids: Eerdmans, 1970), *The Zondervan Bible Pictorial Dictionary,* edited by M. C. Tenney (Grand Rapids: Zondervan, 1963), *The International Standard Bible Encyclopedia* , 4 volumes, edited by Geoffrey Bromiley (Grand Rapids: Eerdmans, 1979–86), and *The Zondervan Pictorial Encyclopedia of the Bible,* 5 volumes, edited by M. C. Tenney (Grand Rapids: Zondervan, 1975)." [35]

A word study is one of the securest ways of assuring the researcher that he will handle the Word of God well in his presentation of the passage. The best interpreter of the Bible is the Bible itself.

Since the Bible is its best interpreter, then the question could be raised, why bother consulting any other work? Simply because although God gave us the Bible as a whole set of canonical writings, He did not at the same time give us a book to

---

[35] MacArthur, J. 1997, c1992. *Rediscovering Expository Preaching.* Word Pub.: Dallas

serve as a key to understanding it. We will learn to appreciate God's revelation more if we have to work in order to make sense of it. The collective works of committed laborers over the centuries to determine what God meant are of great value to us. Studies that give the historical, linguistic, and cultural background for biblical writings not only serve to connect the Bible with space and time but also provide information that most people do not have the opportunity and training to search out. Such written helps, along with interpretations of the Bible itself, are valuable in at least two ways: (1) the researcher of the Word can see where some have gone astray and others have been on target as time tests the views of all, and (2) the illuminating ministry of the Spirit in researchers of the past is preserved for those living in succeeding generations. These individuals who have labored diligently to unfold the meaning of the Master in His manual, the Bible, should be considered.

MacArthur states, "the following hermeneutic axioms will prove helpful to the expositor:

1. *The checking habit.* Check a view and all its details in reliable sources by specialists. On details of history, consult dependable sources on history. For geography, look to experts in geography and for customs, look to experts in customs. On word

meaning, go to better lexicons, thoroughly researched commentaries, etc. Above all, avoid leaning on weak sources, i.e., nonspecialists who themselves should have depended on reliable sources, but for one reason or another have not done so. Checking with genuine rather than pseudo experts applies in every area—on parables, prophecy, typology, etc. It can even be fruitful for blocks of Scripture. " [36] Works specializing on a shorter portion may provide help that commentaries on the whole Bible do not cover as thoroughly. "Concentrated studies deal with such things as creation, the flood, Abraham, the tabernacle, Psalm 25 , the trial and death of Jesus, His resurrection, Romans 6–8 , 1 Corinthians 13 , Hebrews 11 , Revelation 2–3 , 20 , and 21–22 . Topical works discuss marriage, divorce, angels, spiritual warfare, the New Age Movement, and more.

Some resources provide annotated bibliographies on Bible matters. Such helps are very valuable.

2. *The verification principle.* Probe for biblical validation that a duty is obligatory for all times and not just for a particular biblical character. Use other principles to view a matter from every possible angle. To illustrate, God's command to Jacob to "leave this land" (Gen. 31:15), i.e., leave Haran to return to Canaan, is

---

[36] MacArthur, J. 1997, c1992. *Rediscovering Expository Preaching.* Word Pub.: Dallas

inapplicable to a Christian today who is his own person in his own situation. The general principle may be gleaned that God willingly directs a believer, a truth verifiable in other Scriptures. But Genesis 31 does not give him marching orders to do something like go AWOL from military service or leave California for another state. God's will regarding each believer's exact movements depend on a variety of considerations.

3. *The regulation principle.* Scripture, and not experience, regulates doctrine. Pastoral expositors should direct God's sheep to concentrate on what the Great Shepherd says in His Word properly interpreted. Any claim that the Bible plus an experience provide a norm to depend on should be evaluated from the criteria of God's Bureau of Standards, His Word." [37]

This discussion has not treated every important hermeneutical rule, but it has touched on the ones most crucial to a faithful ministry in the Word. When skillfully used, these will assist biblical heralds of God in getting the truth from the Word that God would have them proclaim to others.

The final need to be discussed along with *exercising commitment to context* and *exploring the glamour of the grammar*, and *extensive working on words is* the *employing of an exegesis.*

---

[37] MacArthur, J. 1997, c1992. *Rediscovering Expository Preaching.* Word Pub.: Dallas

Exegesis is the exploring and exposing of the text in the original languages of the Scripture, Greek in the New Testament and Hebrew and Aramaic in the Old Testament. The focus is on distracting knowledge from the original text and not the other translations. Preaching and teaching done in this form is known as expository proclamation.

The exegetical preacher/teacher must have a comprehensive and clear understanding of the passage being studied before creating the procedure for presenting his understanding to the congregation. This is not possible without the guidance of the Spirit of God in the exegete's research. Guidance provides for proper meaning and modeling of the text. Apart from it, the implication and application of the text is equivocated.

"Since God is a God of order (1 Cor. 14:33, 40) and rational creatures created in His image and regenerated by His Spirit are capable of grasping divine logic, the leading of the Spirit in exegetical study will be in accord with divine reason accessible to the exegete." [38]

This process is an inclusive study method. It integrates a study of individual words, their backgrounds, their derivation, their usage, their synonyms, their antonyms, their figurative usages, and

---

[38] MacArthur, J. 1997, c1992. *Rediscovering Expository Preaching* . Word Pub.: Dallas

other lexical aspects that provide specific understanding of the flow of thought intended in the Scripture. Through this process, the intended message of the author can be ensured to be expressed.

The central idea can sometimes be found at a single point in the text. It is important to remember that in normal writings, whether Hebrew, Greek, or English, the main thought of a paragraph is not always found in its first sentence. As in any in-depth study of literature, it is important to identify the main thought or focus of a section. After this it is imperative to make that the main focus of the message. A few examples will clarify.

"1 Tim. 4:6–16. The main thought of 1 Tim. 4:6–16 is in verse 16, where Paul states, "Take heed unto thyself, and unto your doctrine." This is central to the entire passage. It helps if the expositor and his audience are aware of this principal thought from the very beginning of a message. It helps them piece the rest of the passage together. The first thought, "take heed unto thyself," is developed in 4:6–10. The latter, "and unto the doctrine," is the essence of 4:11–15. The impact is enhanced when one realizes that this is a twofold emphasis elsewhere in both 1 Timothy and Titus. These are two key reminders for all church leaders.

Gal. 6:1–10. The proposed chapter and paragraph divisions in Gal. 6:1–10 cause two problems. First, the chapter break makes it easy to study these verses separately from the verses immediately before. One may miss the relationship of these verses to walking in the Spirit and evidencing the fruit of the Spirit. The second problem occurs if one observes the paragraph separation of both Greek and English texts that set verses 6–10 off from verses 1–5. With the passage divided in half, the uniting thought of the entire passage in verse 10, "let us do good to all men, and especially unto those who are of the household of faith," will probably go unnoticed. Another result of such a division is an obscuring of the close relationship between the three parallel commands and cautions found in 6:1–8.

1 Pet. 5:1–11. The main thought of 1 Pet. 5:1–11 is in the middle of verse 5. Verses 1–5 revolve about the command toward one another to "clothe yourselves with humility" in verse 5. This responsibility is applied first to leaders (5:2–4) and then to those who are led (5:5a). Once again, the new paragraph indicated by the texts at verse 6 should not cause the expositor to separate 5:6–11 from the first five verses. They are inseparably connected in thought and emphasis. This is evident in the references to "humility" in the middle of verse 5 and God's giving grace to "the humble" in the last part of verse 5 and the command "to humble oneself" under God's mighty hand in verse 6. The central thought of the message should somehow reflect the need for humility in attitude and service.

82

Matthew 5–7. In the "Sermon on the Mount" recorded in Matthew 5–7, Jesus laid a foundation in 5:1–16 upon which He built in 5:17–20. Verse 20 contains the key for understanding the verses that follow. Jesus there said, "That except your righteousness shall exceed the righteousness of the scribes and Pharisees, you shall in no case enter into the kingdom of heaven." In the verses immediately following (5:21–48), He showed them how their righteousness must exceed that of the scribes. In 6:1–18 He described ways their righteousness must exceed that of the Pharisees.

Zech. 4:1–14. The central idea of the Zech. 4:1–14 is doubtlessly found in 4:6 where the angel says, "This is the word of the LORD to Zerubbabel saying, 'Not by might nor by power, but by My Spirit,' says the LORD of hosts." This principle is given pictorially in 4:1–5, and its results are described in 4:7–10.

Zech. 3:1–10. The central idea in Zechariah 3 is found in the statement, "Behold, I have caused thine iniquity to pass" (3:4). This is expanded later in the statement, "I will remove the iniquity of that land in one day" (3:9). As in Zechariah 4, the picture is given in (3:1–5), and the further description is in (3:6–10)." [39]

---

[39] MacArthur, J. 1997, c1992. *Rediscovering Expository Preaching.* Word Pub.: Dallas

The central idea is sometimes found in a "sandwich-type" structure. Many examples of this structure exist both in broad and restricted contexts.

"1 Corinthians 12–14. First Cor. 12:31–14:1 provides an example of a sandwich-type structure in a broad context. Paul ends the twelfth chapter with the command to "covet earnestly the best gifts" (12:31a). The list preceding this command (12:28) indicates the best gifts were "first apostles, second prophets, third teachers.... " Since the number of apostles was limited, the greatest gift available to most local churches was prophecy. The same form of the verb for "covet earnestly" comes again in 14:1 with the command to "*desire* spiritual gifts, but especially that you may prophesy" (emphasis added). This is a very slight variation of the same command. Sandwiched between those two commands is the thought best described by Paul as a more excellent way, the pursuit for love. The central thought sandwiched between 1 Cor. 12:31 and 14:1 is that the church is to pursue the greater gifts, but in so doing is to manifest the spirit of love described in chapter 13 .

Hebrews 10–12. Hebrews 10:32–12:1 provides another "sandwich" example in a larger context. Chapter 10 ends with the reminder of "the former days, in which … ye endured" (10:32) and the present days, when "ye have need of patience" (10:36). This is followed by what is known as "the faith chapter" (Hebrews 11).

The chapter division is really "an interruption to the thought" since the sense in chapter 11 "flows directly out of 10:35–39 " and then flows naturally into chapter 12 ." [40] "The thought continues in 12:1–7 with the reminder that we are to "run with endurance the race that is set before us" and are to fix our eyes on Jesus, "Looking ... who ... endured the cross" and "consider Him who endured such contradiction" (12:1–3). The author then writes that "If ye endure chastening (12:7)," in order words, it is for discipline that you endure. A message communicated in chapter 11, sandwiched (as it were) between the closing verses of chapter 10 and the opening verses of chapter 12, is that a genuine faith is one which endures. This is evident both in the admonition on either side of this chapter and in most of the examples within the chapter itself." [41]

Once the central idea is revealed through the research process the preacher/teacher is now ready to move to the other necessary stages of building the message.

[40] James Moffatt, *A Critical and Exegetical Commentary on the Epistle to the Hebrews*, International Critical Commentaries (reprint, Edinburgh: T. & T. Clark, 1968), 158; cf. 156, 192.
[41] MacArthur, J. 1997, c1992. *Rediscovering Expository Preaching.* Word Pub.: Dallas

"Reflecting On the Passage"

The next process for the presenter after reading and researching the passage is to reflect on the passage. This process of study is better known as "meditation." Meditation does not involve putting your mind in neutral and allowing it to walk and wander in your thinking. It is a thinking process that is centered upon a particular pattern of thought. Meditation entails focusing the mind on one subject, involving reason, imagination, and emotions. Concentrated meditation on the truths of God's Word weaves those truths into the fabric of our lives. The presenter must constantly *feed* and *feast* his mind on the Word.

The meditation process is perhaps one of the most vital and valuable steps in the preparation of the message. This is a period of time during which the mind is able to incorporate the previously gained information into an interpretation of the text. Theologically, a great deal hangs upon meditating over material. To obtain a proper exposition of the text, one must view the passage from the mind of God. Meditation helps one to arrive at this juncture and equips him to speak as the mouth of God. Prayerful meditation is the process.

Many messengers of the Word of God can attest to the fact that after periods of detachment from study books and even from the Bible, the truth that the Lord would have shared with His people is pounded in the heart. Sometimes the interpretational truth comes while walking, riding, dreaming, or even upon awakening from a good night's sleep. It comes from meditation.

Meditation should be deliberate, but it should also be casual. The mind should be disciplined so that it can be called upon to thoughtfully digest the material with which it has been saturated and yet allow the sub-conscious mind an opportunity to do its work. The man of God should prayerfully ask God to increase this special ability of the mind so that he can truly be "redeeming the time."

Meditation may be defined as a private devotional act, consisting in deliberate reflection upon some spiritual truth or mystery, accompanied by mental prayer and by acts of the affection and of the will, especially formation of resolutions as to future conduct. "Meditation is a duty that ought to be attended to by all who wish well to their spiritual interests. It should be *conscious, close,* and *continuous* (Psalm 1:2; Psalm 119:97). The *subjects* that ought more especially to engage the Christian mind are: the works of creation (Psalm 19:1-6); the perfections of God (Deut. 32:4); the character, office, and work of Christ (Hebrews 12:2-3); the office and operations of the Holy Spirit (John 15-16); the dispensations of Providence (Psalm 97:1-2); the precepts and promises of God's words (Psalm 119); the value, powers, and immortality of the soul (Mark 8:36); the depravity of our nature, and the grace of God in our salvation, etc." [42]

King David was labeled by God as a man that was after His heart. One of the reasons he was given this prestigious title was because he continued to reflect on the Word of God. In presenting the purity of the passage, the preacher/teacher must reach the heart of God. Reflecting on the Word of God is a sure and sound pathway that will lead to the heart of God. Dedicated reflection on the passage combined with detailed researching of the passage will help in illuminating the central idea intended by the Bible Author Himself.

---

[42] New Unger's Bible Dictionary, Meditation

Chapter Four

The Packaging of the Passage

After the preparatory work of supplication and studying has been activated and applied, the next step for the presenter is the packaging of the passage. This is the process of bringing together the studied and supplicated material in a form to be presented. This process is known as "the art of exposition." Building a message requires as much preparation as building a literal structure. It would be foolish to begin building a large office complex without first having carefully laid plans. Yet many times a message is put together without any planning or preparation. Often this is attributed to laziness. Laziness is not synonymous with being "instant in season." The packaging of the passage is a simple homiletic sequence for building the structure of the message. An exegete is like a diver bringing up pearls from the ocean bed; an expositor is like the jeweler who arrays them in orderly fashion and in proper relation to each other.

The packaging of the passage process includes a focus on titles, outlines, introductions, illustrations, and conclusions. The message flows, although it may not logically flow at this time as it will in the main body, from the raw materials developed by an exegesis of the passage to the ready material designed for the exposition of the passage which will convict, compel, challenge, and comfort the listener. During this process, the listener should not be forgotten. The expositor, as he pulls the cover off the text, must keep in mind the congregation as the message is formed.

F. B. Meyer offers this advice when thinking of the listeners and what sermonic form the message will take: "There are five considerations that must be met in every successful message. There should be an appeal to the Reason, to the Conscience, to the Imagination, to the Emotions, and to the Will; and for each of these there is no method so serviceable as systematic exposition." [43]

Listened below are some key components to keep in mind as the message is being packaged, or put together:

1. The Scripture should be the continuous establishment of the message.
2. The Scripture should be carefully examined to extract the message.
3. The Scripture should be correctly expressed in the message.
4. The Scripture should be the clear explanation of the message.

---

[43] F. B. Meyer, *Expository Preaching Plans and Methods* (New York: George H. Duran, 1912), 100.

"The Sketch of the Passage"

There is a need to determine not only the central idea of a passage but also the outline that reflects the thinking of the author. The outline is a sketch or skeleton of the passage being studied and the meat is the substance of the passage being studied. In my sermon outline books, volume 1 and 2, I call this outlining *"Bones From The Pulpit."* These two volumes contain homiletically outlined passages from the Bible that I have shared in the sanctuary of First Baptist Church Main Street, North Little Rock, Arkansas. These "bones" reflect my thinking as I exegete the passage.

Why is structure to the message important? "God is not the author of confusion, but some preachers are, and they do it in God's name. Whether the congregation identifies each point or sub-point in the outline is not that important. But the presenter must know where he is going and how to get there. Once the theme has been announced, there must be a *development* of the material in an interesting and practical way.

Most message outlines would consist of:

- An introduction
- A statement of purpose (proposition, "big idea")

- Two or more main points (development)
- Conclusion.

The artist studies anatomy so that his painting of the human figure will be more realistic. What the skeleton is to the body, the outline is to the message: it is not obvious, but it had better be there.

The structure of the message depends primarily on the development of the material in the biblical text. It is an unpardonable sin to develop an outline and then force it upon a passage of Scripture.

The structure also depends on the statement of purpose. The student must *find* and *focus* on this statement. The statement of purpose in one sermon may have three main points and each of them being a *result*. The statement of purpose in another may have four main points and each of them being a *reason* rather than a result.

Finally, the structure should take into account the total "preaching pattern" of the minister. There is always a need for variety. The itinerant preacher can use the same homiletical approach because he changes congregations; but the resident pastor must change approaches because he speaks to the same congregation week after week. To use "reasons" or "results" or

92

"lessons" every Sunday would make our preaching predictable and rob the message of power.

Each preacher has his own distinctive style, and this is as it should be. The beginning preacher would do well to submit himself to the disciplines of the homiletical rules until he has discovered and developed his own unique approach. You can break the rules once the rules have broken you.

Organization in a sermon must be a servant and not a master. The preacher must live with the same tension that the architect battles - form vs. function. "What a marvelous outline!" is not the highest compliment a preacher can receive. Far better for us to hear, "You showed us the Lord today, and he met our need." [44]

The outline needs to be grammatically parallel and correct in style to ensure a logical, concise presentation of the material. By learning to identify and to integrate the researched material in outline form, the preacher/teacher is better able to present his message.

Sketching the passage will serve as a great benefit to the presenter providing that he doesn't become a prisoner or slave to it. He should attempt to memorize his outline and then be flexible

---

[44] Wiersbe, W. W., & Wiersbe, D. 1986. *The elements of preaching: The art of biblical preaching clearly and simply presented.* Tyndale House Publishers: Wheaton, Ill.

enough that he can discard his outline if God should so lead. The preacher/teacher needs to be prepared, and he needs to keep on preparing himself so that his message comes forth freely and forcefully. A good outline can certainly help him to achieve this. I prefer to use sub points in my outline as hooks to hang my thoughts. These sub points helps in keeping my thoughts on target with the text.

The following are some helpful principles in preparing an outline that can be used in sketching the passage during the packaging process:

1. Declare the message in the outline. The outline is useless if the meaning and message of the text are not reflected. Make sure that the outline reflects the thought pattern of the writer. Remember that the important thing is not the prettiness of the outline, but the purity of the outline.

2. Dig out the outline from the message. Don't put together an outline from your human wisdom and try to force it to fix the Holy Word. Instead of pushing the outline into the passage, pull the outline from the passage.

3. Demand that the passage speaks to you and not you to the passage. Don't try to create an outline by speaking things in the passage that do not exist. Remain true to the text and allow the outline to flow from it.

As the preacher/teacher discovers the outline for the passage using the prescribed principles, the results will look something like this:

Example 1: 1 Thessalonians (1:2) "We give thanks to God always for you all, making mention of you in our prayers..."

1. Declare the message in the outline. The main thought in this chapter revolves around the statement, "We give thanks" (1:2). Thanksgiving should be declared in the outline.

2. Dig out the outline from the message with thanksgiving in mind. What is being said about "thanksgiving"? It is given.

3. Demand that the passage speaks to you about thanksgiving.

   A. The Person being Thanked- God

   B. The Period of the Thanksgiving- always

   C. The Purpose of the Thanksgiving- for you all

   D. The Place of the Thanksgiving- in my prayers.

Example 2: 1 Thessalonians 1: (2-4) "We give thanks to God always for you all, making mention of you in our prayers, (3) remembering without ceasing your work of faith, labour of love, and patience of hope in our Lord Jesus Christ in the sight of God and our Father, (4) knowing, brethren beloved, your election of God." Viewing this passage with "thanksgiving" as the central idea and using the participles (words that are used as verbs and adjectives) that describe the thanksgiving, an outline may be developed that would look like this:

A.   The Manner of the Thanksgiving- we give

B.   The Moment of the Thanksgiving- always

C.   The Meditation of Thanksgiving- prayers (praying)

D.   The Motive for Thanksgiving- your work.

Example 3: 2 Timothy (4:1-4) "I charge you therefore before God and the Lord Jesus Christ, who shall judge the quick and the dead at His appearing and His kingdom; (2) Preach the word, be instant in season, out of season: reprove, rebuke, exhort, with all longsuffering and doctrine. (3) For the time will come when they will not endure sound doctrine, but after their own lusts, shall they heap to themselves teachers, having itching ears: (4) and they shall turn away their ears from the truth, and be turned unto fables." Viewing this passage with "a charge to preach" as the central idea, an outline may look like this:

1. Divine Charge (1): This charge is divine because the...
    A. Presence of God is divine - "I charge you before God and the Lord Jesus Christ.
    B. Position of God is divine - "who will judge..."

2. Defined Charge (2): Paul shares with Timothy what the charge is, a...
    A. Preaching charge is given - "preach the word..."
    B. Preparation charge is given - "be ready in season and out of season."

3. Desperate Charge (3,4): This is why the charge is urgent; there will be a ...
    A. Period of not hearing the Word - "the time will come..."
    B. Problem of not heeding to the Word - "turn their ears away from the truth..."

The following sketches are excerpts from my two books, *Bones from the Pulpit Volumes 1 & 2*. These outlines may serve as practice tools as you endeavor to enhance your outlining skills. These sample outlines use alliteration (the rhyming of sounds). The alliteration serves as a tool for memorization, helpful to both the presenter and the people. Never sacrifice accuracy for the sake of alliteration. Preachers who are addicted to alliteration like to find words in their text that begin with the same letter and somehow tie them together in an outline. Sometimes this approach will work (e.g., *flee, follow, fight*, in the KJV of 1 Tim. 6:11, 12), but usually it leads to a forced outline based on bad exegesis.

There is no substitute for knowledge of the original languages to set you free from bondage to a translation. Many fine basic tools are available today so that even the person with little knowledge of Hebrew and Greek may secure the technical help needed.

The careful student of the Word will always consult several reliable translations, as well as the original, just to make certain he is on the main highway and not on a dangerous detour.

One test of the validity of the sermon outline is this: Can you preach it from any reliable translation? If your outline is limited to one translation, then you may be building on the accidentals and not the essentials. One exception to this rule would be when a translation gives a unique coloring to a phrase or a verse, and you point this out to your listeners. Just be sure that, with all its uniqueness, the translation is still accurate.

There are various methods that may be used in the outlining process; the important object in whatever process chosen is to remain true to the text. As you view the following outlines, notice the application of the three aforementioned principles suggested for sketching the passage. I use this method religiously as I prepare messages and have found it very helpful in preparation for the presentation of the purity of the passage. Here is the application for review:

1. Declare the message in the outline. The outline is useless if the meaning and message of the text are not reflected. Make sure that the outline reflects the thought pattern of the writer. Remember that the important thing is not the prettiness of the outline, but the purity of the outline.

2. Dig out the outline from the message. Don't put together an outline from your human wisdom and try to force it to fix the Holy Word. Instead of pushing the outline into the passage, pull the outline from the passage.

3. Demand that the passage speaks to you and not you to the passage. Don't try to create an outline by speaking things in the passage that does not exist. Remain true to the text and allow the outline to flow from it.

These outlines were developed from various passages of the Bible using this same method:

SUBJECT: Consider Christ
SCRIPTURE: Hebrews 3:1-2

SERMON OUTLINE:
1. Holy Citizenship (1a)
    A. Salvation
    B. Sanctification
    C. Spirit-filled
2. Heavenly Calling (1b)
    A. Spiritual blessings in heavenly places
    B. Spiritual battle with high powers
    C. Spiritual boldness to hold your position
3. High Position of our Confession (1c, 2)
    A. Supreme messenger of God
    B. Supreme mediator of God
    C. Supreme man of God

SERIES:

SUBJECT: When I See Jesus

SCRIPTURE: 1John 3:2

_SERMON OUTLINE:

1. Glorious Coming of Christ (2a)

    A. Fullness of glory

    B. Faithful will be gathered

    C. Forgotten will be grieved

2. Guaranteed Change of His Children (2b)

    A. Forgiven by God

    B. Faith in God

    C. Future with God

3. Great Celebration in the City (2c)

    A. Family celebration

    B. Farewell celebration

    C. Forever celebration

NOTES:

SERIES:

SUBJECT: Do Business Till I Come

SCRIPTURE: Luke 19:11-27

SERMON OUTLINE:

1. Recruitment of the Stewards (12, 13)

    A. Recruiter

    B. Recruitees

    C. Reason

2. Responsibility of the Stewards (13b)

    A. Received the same count

    B. Received the same calling

    C. Received the same command

3. Rewards of the Stewards (15-27)

    A. Recognized publicly

    B. Ruling position

    C. Return was profitless

NOTES:

SERIES:

SUBJECT: The Fall into Divers Temptations

SCRIPTURE: James 1:2-4, 12

SERMON OUTLINE:

1. Directions Before the Fall (2)

> A. Citizens of the fall
>
> B. Counsel concerning the fall
>
> C. Coming of the fall

2. Developments During the Fall (3, 4)

> A. Wisdom about God
>
> B. Waiting on God
>
> C. Wholeness in God

3. Dividends After the Fall (12)

> A. Blessed man
>
> B. Benefited man
>
> C. Bragging man

NOTES:

SERIES:

SUBJECT: Soul Food

SCRIPTURE: John 6:31-35

SERMON OUTLINE:

1. Heavenly Food (31-33a)

    A. Presence of God

    B. Possessed by God

    C. Person of God

2. Healthy Food (33b)

    A. Prepares the soul

    B. Purifies the soul

    C. Peace to the soul

3. Holding Food (34-35)

    A. Powerful proclamation

    B. Permanent provision

    C. Position in paradise

NOTES:

SERIES:

SUBJECT: God Is Still On the Throne

SCRIPTURE: Psalm 93:1-5

SERMON OUTLINE:

1. His Sovereignty (1a)

    A. Reverenced master

    B. Reigning messiah

    C. Robed in majesty

2. His Stability (1b-2)

    A. Planet Earth

    B. Paradise of eternity

    C. Person being everlasting

3. His Strength (3-5)

    A. Proverb

    B. Promises

    C. Purity

NOTES:

SERIES:

SUBJECT: A Family of Dry Bones

SCRIPTURE: Ezekiel 37:1-10

SERMON OUTLINE:

1. Family's Dreadful Condition (1-2)

    A. Down

    B. Divided

    C. Dry

2. Father's Divine Concern (3)

    A. Suffering

    B. Satisfaction

    C. Soul

3. Formula for Direct Cure (4)

    A. Revelation of God's person

    B. Releasing of God's power

    C. Revival of God's people

NOTES:

SERIES:

SUBJECT: Tree-like Christianity

SCRIPTURE: Psalm 1:1-3

SERMON OUTLINE:

1. Separated from the World (1)

    A. Listen to ungodly counsel

    B. Linger with ungodly company

    C. Laugh with ungodly critics

2. Saturated with the Word (2)

    A. Delight in the word

    B. Diet on the word

    C. Doer of the word

3. Situated by the Water (3)

    A. Permanent

    B. Productive

    C. Protected

    D. Prosper

NOTES:

SERIES:

SUBJECT: Thank God for the Gospel

SCRIPTURE: Romans 1:16-19

SERMON OUTLINE:

1. Redeeming Power (16)

    A. Person of the Gospel

    B. Power of the Gospel

    C. Purpose of the Gospel

2. Revealing Power (17)

    A. Pure nature of the Master

    B. Polluted nature of man

    C. Potential of man

3. Rescuing Power (18, 19)

    A. Penalty of sin

    B. Power of sin

    C. Presence of sin

NOTES:

SERIES:

SUBJECT: A Spiritual Soldier

SCRIPTURE: 2 Timothy 2:3-5

SERMON OUTLINE:

1. Spiritual Endurance (3)

    A. Patient soldier

    B. Praying soldier

    C. Persevere as a soldier

2. Spiritual Engagement (4)

    A. Spiritual fight

    B. Spiritual focus

    C. Spiritual father

3. Spiritual Encouragement (5)

    A. Compete in the race

    B. Crown being rewarded

    C. Competing by the rules

NOTES:

SUBJECT: What We Have in Christ

SCRIPTURE: Ephesians 1:1-6

SERMON OUTLINE:

1. Significance (1, 2)

    A. Followers of Christ

    B. Faithful in Christ

    C. Favor of Christ

2. Sufficiency (3)

    A. Producer of all things

    B. Possessor of all things

    C. Provider of all things

3. Security (4-6)

    A. Chose us in the beginning

    B. Cleaned us with His blood

    C. Crowned us with a birthright

NOTES:

SERIES:

SUBJECT: The Christ of Christmas

SCRIPTURE: Luke 1:26-38

SERMON OUTLINE:

1. Mother of Christ (28:38)

    A. Favor of God

    B. Fellowship with God

    C. Faithful to God

2. Majesty of Christ (35)

    A. Nature of His birth

    B. Name of the baby

    C. Need for the baby

3. Mission of Christ (31-33)

    A. Free man from sin

    B. Fill man with His spirit

    C. Fashion man after His son

NOTES:

SERIES:

SUBJECT: The Christ at the Pool

SCRIPTURE: John 5:1-9

SERMON OUTLINE:

1. Compassionate Christ (6)
   A. Homeless in his position
   B. Helpless in his power
   C. Hopeless in his predicament

2. Challenging Christ (6-8)
   A. Walk in love
   B. Walk in the light
   C. Walk in the law

3. Changing Christ (8)
   A. Worldly ways
   B. Wicked words
   C. Wishful wants

NOTES:

SERIES:

SUBJECT: Because of His Mercy

SCRIPTURE: Lamentations 3:21-24

SERMON OUTLINE:

1. Fortress in God (22)

    A. Shielding power

    B. Sustaining power

    C. Story with power

2. Forgiveness of God (22a)

    A. Saves sinners

    B. Sanctifies saints

    C. Stronger than sin

3. Faithfulness of God

    A. Surplus of mercy

    B. Schedule for mercy

    C. Soul full of mercy

NOTES:

SERIES:

SUBJECT: Richness of His Mercy (2)

SCRIPTURE: Ephesians 2:1-7

SERMON OUTLINE:

1. Dark Past of Man (1-3)

   A. Dead in sins

   B. Disobedient spirit

   C. Desires were selfish

2. Divine Passion of the Master (4-7)

   A. Degree of His love

   B. Distribution of His love

   C. Destination of His love

3. Deliverance Power of His Mercy (8)

   A. Delivered by grace

   B. Dividends in Glory

   C. Declare His goodness

NOTES:

SUBJECT: God's Rainbow in the Sky

SCRIPTURE: Genesis 9: 12-17

SERMON OUTLINE:

---

1. Colors of the Rainbow (12-14)

    A. Purple- royalty

    B. Blue- residence

    D. Green- resurrection

    E. Yellow- radiance

    F. Orange- repentance

    G. Red- redemption

2. Coverage by the Rainbow (15, 16)

    A. Promised coverage

    B. Perpetual coverage

    C. Price for the coverage

3. Cause for the Rainbow

    A. Storm of sin

    B. Sign from the Savior

    C. Serenity for the saved

"The Subject of the Passage"

Title selection can be a nuisance to the presenter if he is not careful. Many expositors spend timeless labor trying to create a fancy and famous title to only yield the creation of a false and foolish testimony. The subject of the passage is important and should be given special attention to express the essence of the message. Here are some principles to ponder when selecting the subject of the passage.

The subject of the passage should be a reflection of the passage itself. The presenter must be cautious not to allow the title to transcend the text. The subject that surpasses the Scripture begins with the wrong focus and is dangerous to the listener. The presenter must be committed to a subject that will reflect the content of the message. The title should be served as an appetizer and not the main course.

"A study of the titles given to 1 Pet. 2:1–8 which states: Wherefore laying aside all malice, and all guile, and hypocrisies, and envies, and all evil speaking,[2] As newborn babes, desire the sincere milk of the word, that ye may grow thereby: [3] If so be ye have tasted that the Lord *is* gracious.[4] To whom coming, *as unto* a living stone, disallowed indeed of men, but chosen of God, *and* precious,[5] Ye also, as lively stones, are built up a spiritual house, an holy priesthood, to offer up spiritual sacrifices, acceptable to God by Jesus Christ.[6] Wherefore also it is contained in the scripture, Behold, I lay in Sion a chief corner stone, elect, and precious: and he that believeth on him shall not be confounded.[7] Unto you therefore which believe *he is* precious: but unto them which be disobedient, the stone which the builders disallowed, the same is made the head of the corner, [8] And a stone of stumbling, and a rock of offence, *even to them* which stumble at the word, being disobedient: whereunto also they were appointed., reveals that despite the fact that the rest of the verses speak primarily of Christ and not the believer, the focus is often placed on the spiritual sacrifices of verse 5. Yet the focus of even verse 5 is on Him. Believers are "living stones" (2:5) only because of their relationship to Him who is by quality a "living stone" (2:4). In addition, the only reason why the spiritual sacrifices please God is their channeling "through Jesus Christ" (2:5). In the choice of a title, then, the focus must be on the person of Christ rather than the work of the believer, on Him to whom the believer continually comes (2:4). Only then, secondarily, is attention drawn to the believer's relationship to and service for Him." [45]

---

[45] MacArthur, J. 1997, c1992. *Rediscovering expository preaching*. Word Pub.: Dallas

117

From this study, a simple outline can be formed that will help to form the subject. For instance, with the following outline, a subject dealing with the believer's relationship can be formed:

1. Our relationship to the Scripture — 2:1–3

2. Our relationship to the Saint — 2:4–8

3. Our relationship to the Sinner — 2:9–10

Another subject can be formed from the outline concerning the Christian:

1. The Primacy of the Christian (thirst for the Word) - 2:1-3

2. The Position of the Christian (relationship to Christ)- 2:4-8

3. The Privilege of the Christian (proclamation) - 2:9-10

Whatever the titles may be, they must reflect the meaning of the passage and hence the contents of the message.

"The Start of the Passage"

One of the most important points of the presentation is the introduction. If a preacher/teacher fails to gain his audience's attention with a captivating introduction, he has probably lost them for the rest of the message. The introduction to the message is like the opening jump ball at a basketball game, the opening kickoff at a football game, the opening pitch at a baseball game; it is where things get started. It is the first impression that is often the last impression.

The preacher/teacher must realize that the introduction is very important to the rest of the message. If the preacher/teacher does not get a grip of his congregation's attention within the first five minutes of a message, chances are they will not grasp much of the rest of the message. The human mind can think at the rate of 750 words a minute. You can only speak about 150 words a minute. Therefore, the introduction must captivate the listeners mind as quickly as possible; otherwise they are going to be thinking about what they want to do as soon as you shut-up.

The introduction should be made a matter of prayer just as the other part of the message is made a matter of prayer. The presenter should rely on the Holy Spirit to direct and deliver his thoughts as he prepares the introduction. Ask Him to help you to be sensitive to the needs of the congregation you are going to share with. He knows their needs better than you do.

It is important to understand what the purpose of the introduction is. How does the introduction relate the other parts of the message? The introduction of the message is where the presenter *presents* his case. The body of the message is where the presenter *proves* his case. The conclusion is where the presenter *pleads* his case. In the introduction the *declaration* is approached and asserted; in the body the *documentation* is amplified and applied; and in the conclusion the *decision* is asked and appealed. When the message is introduced, the presenter is trying to convince the congregation that what he has to say is important and exciting. If he does a bad job of communicating this fact, then he shouldn't expect the listeners to be excited about what he has to say.

"Someone has said that the introduction to a sermon may be likened to the prelude to a poem, the preface to a book, the portico to a building, or the preamble to the statement of a case in court. The prelude introduces us to a poem, suggests its method and meaning or message. The preface to a book also does that.... An introduction, then, must introduce." [46]

The following are reasons why the introduction to the message is important.

---

[46] G. Campbell Morgan, *Preaching* (reprint, Grand Rapids: Baker, 1974), 81.

The introduction:

1. Engages the audience's attention to focus on the messenger and his message.
2. Enhances the audience's acceptance to favor the messenger and his message.
3. Elevates the audience's anticipation to feast from the message by the messenger.
4. Expresses the scriptural significance of the message.
5. Exposes the presenter's pathway for the message.

The preacher/teacher should use his ingenuity and imagination in developing the introduction. Creativity is a plus. There are many ideas available for the presenter that can be gained by a commitment to the reading of current and historical insights. Listed below are several sources that may serve as introduction material.

1. Current events

2. Historical events

3. Life stories

4. Famous quotations

5. Humor

6. TV shows

7. Sporting events

8. Personal experiences

9. References to writings by other authors

10. Religious and secular songs

11. Metaphorical questions directed to the audience

12. Fictional stories

13. Contemporary parables.

Where does the introduction fall in the message preparation process? There is the advantage of knowing what message you will be introducing when the message is completed and the introduction is at the end of the process. This is the process I use. I have discovered that it is difficult to introduce what you don't know.

"The Shutting of the Passage"

The conclusion or "shutting up" of the message is the process of bringing everything to an end. It is the process of closing the door to the message that was opened in the introduction. Some preachers/teachers make the statement "I'm closing now" and just go on and on with the message. It often makes the listener wonder how many more doors he will have to shut before he really closes. The conclusion should be the conclusion. Here are some methods that may be used to bring a conclusion to the message:

1. Summarize the content of the message. The message can be brought to a close by reviewing the major points of the message.
2. Summon a challenge to the message. The congregation can be challenged to move from where they are to where God desires for them to be in their spirituality.
3. Stir up a commitment to the message. The conclusion can motivate the listener to make a commitment as it relates to the message presented.
4. Spread the comfort of the message. The door to the message may be closed by sharing words or expressions of comfort as a conclusion.

The following are some "do not's" to watch for in writing the conclusion to a message:

1. Do not *introduce* new material to the message in the conclusion.

2. Do not *impose* difficulty to the message in the conclusion.

3. Do not *insert* new demands to the message in the conclusion.

4. Do not *increase* the length of the message by adding the conclusion.

5. Do not *irritate* the listener by not concluding when you say you are concluding.

Many messages, especially when delivered during a worship service, usually conclude with what is know as an invitation to Christian discipleship, which refers to an invitation to a sinner to salvation or a saint to church membership. When the message is concluded with an invitation to salvation or church membership, several methods of closure can be used. The presenter can ask the congregation to stand and invite those to come to the altar who would like to make a commitment to salvation or church membership. The presenter can also ask those who desire to make the commitment today to fill out the decision card in the pew and give it to one of the counselors at the door as they exit. Also, trained counselors can be available after every service in an established prayer room where people can go in response to a concluding appeal. In giving the invitation, do pick up the feelings of those in the throes of decision. Empathize with their fear of embarrassment, of not being able to follow through, of what others will say. Hear the inner voice that tells them this is too hard, or they can wait — it's not important. Don't berate or threaten. Do explain very simply what it is you are asking people to do. If you want them to get up, walk forward, stand at the front, face you, and wait until you have had a prayer, tell them exactly what will happen.

Here are some "Do's and Don'ts" as it relates to the invitation:

- Don't ask them only to raise their hand, and then only to stand, and then only to come forward. This is not to say we should never give an invitation in two steps, but it does mean we must not trick people or make them feel used.
- Do make the meaning of the invitation clear.
- Do wait patiently, giving people time to think and pray, knowing the inner conflicts they may be facing. Sometimes those moments seem agonizingly slow for you, but be patient.
- Don't extend and prolong when there is no response, saying "Just one more verse" twenty times, until the congregation groans inwardly for someone to go forward so you'll stop.

- Do encourage and urge people gently, repeating your invitation once or perhaps twice. But don't preach your sermon again.
- Do give the invitation with conviction, with courage, with urgency, with expectancy. But don't try to take the place of the Holy Spirit.

"The Substance of the Passage"

The developing of the body or main points of the message is referred to as the substance of the passage. It is the meat and the matter of the message that the messenger desires to convey to the congregation. This is a move from the exegesis of the passage to the exposition of the passage. This is a complete process of interpretation of the passage. During this process, the sketch of the passage or outline is revisited for the purpose of ensured continuity with the main thought desired to be presented. It is important to note that during the interpretative processing of the passage, the presenter not only declares the meaning of the passage but he should also defend the meaning of the passage. The presenter, as he echoes a statement, must provide evidence to support the statement. Why should the listeners believe that what you are saying is factual without a presentation of evidence?

The presenter must remember that his prime and principal obligation is to present the purity of the passage and not to please the passion of the people. Inspiration without information can not yield implementation. The presenter should seek to firstly and utmostly inform the listener of the divine truth of the Word and help him to arrive at an understanding. An aggressive and acrobatic effort to generate inspiration without accurate and applicable information only produces what I call "saints on Sunday, and ain'ts on Monday". These are individuals who are excited about living for Jesus for a while, but soon the thrill is gone.

Wiersbe discusses the substance of the message in the following manner. "The purpose of preaching is not simply to discuss a subject, but to achieve an object. A true sermon involves not only explanation but also application. A preacher must not be satisfied merely to instruct the mind; he must also stir the heart and motivate the will to apply God's truth personally.

An outline is not a message any more than a blueprint is a building or a recipe is a meal. What a sick man needs is medicine, not a lecture on health. The object of the sermon will depend on several factors:

- The message of the text.
- The specific needs of the congregation.
- The particular burdens on the pastor's heart.
- The leading of the Spirit of God as the minister meditates and prays.

The pastoral intent and the biblical content must not be divorced. G. Campbell Morgan once wrote in his diary this report of a message he listened to: "Heard a capital sermon with which I did not at all agree, on a text which had no relation to the subject." Even in Morgan's day, a text without a context was still a pretext!" [47] Intent and content are both important ingredients in the message.

During the interpretive process, as the presenter exposes, examines, and explains the points of the outline, the next step is the employing of cross-referencing to each point. Cross-referencing each point will help to expose, expand, and elevate the truth. It also gives credibility to the presented interpretation of the passage which serves as critical and convincing evidence to the listener. By strengthening and supporting the truths of a passage with other Scriptures, the presenter shows that Scripture doesn't contradict itself, but is consistent and concrete in its teaching. A word of warning to the presenter: Make sure that the cross-reference

---

[47] Wiersbe, W. W., & Wiersbe, D. 1986. *The elements of preaching : The art of biblical preaching clearly and simply presented.* Tyndale House Publishers: Wheaton, Ill.

Scriptures being used to support the presented passage are not forced. Those verses should be used in their own context as well as those from the passage being presented.

Many study Bibles have marginal references that are similar to a concordance. However, their connection with the verse to which they are keyed is intentionally less precise. A concordance is based on the occurrence of exact words. Hence, the living creatures in Ezekiel chapter 1 can be traced through Scripture only by means of the phrase "living creatures".

Sometimes the marginal references will be keyed to a particular word, and so will act as a concordance. In many cases, however, they index only related concepts, events, or individuals. For Ezekiel 1:19, a study Bible may have a cross-reference to Revelation 4:7. When the cross-reference passage is looked up, then similar living creatures are discovered. Yet they differ from the cherubs/living creatures in enough particulars to caution the student against immediate or conclusive identification of the two. In Revelation 4:7 the living creatures have the same facial identity as those in Ezekiel 1, but they have six wings each, not four as in Ezekiel. Use of the marginal reference may lead to a possibly related passage, but the passage should be examined to discover the exact nature of the relationship between the two passages on a list of areas for further study.

Both a concordance (whether complete or partial) and the marginal references are the first tools that the Bible student should turn to in dealing with any passage. Both foster familiarization with varied portions of Scriptures and allow the Bible to interpret itself. Develop the habit of consulting them regularly.

Traina warns of those who "fail to take the time to examine each unit to discover its singular meaning, and … therefore frequently make erroneous associations. The result is much faulty interpretation."[48] He adds that "the danger to which attention is being called is the failure to interpret each unit in its own right before blending various units together. If each passage is first expounded as a literary entity, then valid associations will be made, and such associations will be beneficial. But if there occurs an amalgamation of material before each unit is expounded in view of its own context, then errors in exposition will be the inevitable result."[49]

John MacArthur states that "commentaries, lexicons, and concordances are good sources for cross references. Perhaps the best source, however, is *The Treasury of Scripture Knowledge.* It gives extensive cross-references for nearly every verse in the Bible. Its format is similar to marginal references found in most

---

[48] Robert A. Traina, Methodical *Bible Study* (Wilmore, Ky.: Author, 1952), 179–80.
[49] Ibid., 180.

Bibles, but the citations are far more extensive. The book *10,000 Biblical Illustrations* contains another helpful collection of references to aid in using the Bible to explain the Bible." [50]

Cross-referencing causes Scripture to interpret Scripture. The more a truth is illustrated from Scripture, the more it is illuminated and implanted in the hearts of the listeners. The preacher/teacher should also be careful not to use too many cross-reference verses or to spend more time expounding on the cross-reference verses than the main passage. The main passage should always be the star of the message. The cross-references are only the supporting cast.

Once the substance of the passage, the main body, has been constructed and connected, then it must be illustrated. Spurgeon shares the significance and the role of illustrations in his writing. "A building without windows would be a prison rather than a house, for it would be quite dark, and no one would care to take it upon lease; and, in the same way, a discourse without a parable is prosy and dull, and involves a grievous weariness of the flesh.… Our congregations hear us with pleasure when we give them a fair measure of imagery: when an anecdote is being told they rest, take breath, and give play to their imaginations, and thus prepare

---

[50] John Macarthur, *Rediscovering Expository Preaching*, p 291.

131

themselves for the sterner work which lies before them in listening to our profounder expositions." [65]

The following are some helpful questions that one should ask as he takes inventory of the message to be presented to ensure its effectiveness in the life of the listener:

1. Is the message solidly based on Scripture?
2. Does it exalt the Person and work of Jesus Christ?
3. Is the message helpful in meeting the needs of the congregation?
4. Is the theme a timeless truth worth talking about?
5. Is the message organized so that I can preach it clearly and the people understand it easily? Is there a concise and clear statement of purpose? Is there a clear plan of development? Is there practical application that makes the message personal?
6. Are all Scripture references and historical facts accurate?
7. Is the message real to me personally so that I may make it real to others?
8. Does this message fit into the total "preaching plan" for this church and into the context of the church's ministry at this time?

---

[65] C. H. Spurgeon, *Lectures to My Students: Third Series* (reprint, Grand Rapids: Baker, 1977), 2

9. Does the message fit into the ministry of the Church at large and Christ's concern to save a lost world?

10. Is the message worth preaching again?

Chapter Five

The Proclamation of the Passage

After the development of the message through the packaging process the next step is the proclamation process. This is the actual delivery of the finished product. Before the presenter takes the platform, he should make sure that the Word of God is the source and substance of the message. When this is the case, he will be able to walk to the platform to proclaim the message of God with confidence, knowing that diligent study and supplication of the Scripture has been his practice. Preparation is paramount!

The proclamation ministry can be summarized as the communication of God's Word by God's servant to God's people. The communicator must diligently learn how to best communicate the truth to others. Being effective in message delivery requires a certain degree of skill but a lot of practice. Regardless of how good the message may be, if it is poorly delivered it will leave a bad taste in the mouth of the listener. It is like having a flame with no fire, the sun with no heat. Although the doctrine is the most important part of the truth to be heard, the delivery plays an important role in making sure the doctrine is heard.

An intensive study of the New Testament Greek verbs used to describe the communicating of the Word of God will yield the results of three important words. These three most important words are: *euangelizomai*, "to tell the good news"; *kerusso*, "to proclaim like a herald"; and *martureo*, "to bear witness." All three are important in the proclamation ministry.

Jefferson writes about the manner of delivery, "It is surprising how stoutly and stubbornly the churches insist upon preachers knowing how to preach. They will forgive almost everything else, but they will not forgive inability to preach…. No man who knows how to preach with grace and power need stand idle in the market-place a single hour. Churches are scouring the country in search of such a man, and he cannot escape if he would!" [52] Having a preacher who can preach is a hot commodity.

The presenter must learn to fashion his speech appropriately to declare the Gospel with confidence and conviction. He must know when to shout, when to plead, when to whisper, and when to reason? As the preacher/teacher seeks to present the purity of the passage, he will discover that delivery is vital in being successful in the proclamation ministry. The

---

[52] Charles Edward Jefferson, *The Minister As Prophet* (New York: Crowell, 1905), 17.

following chapters will share principles concerning how successful delivery may be achieved.

"Delivering with Purpose"

When the presenter of the message is conscious of the fact that he is delivering a message from the Lord, for the Lord, then he can deliver with the proper perspective. He must constantly be aware of the reality that he is God's representative. The Apostle Paul describes the messenger of God as an ambassador. An ambassador is someone who receives a message from a higher authority and delivers that message to the designated personnel. The presenter is the ambassador, God is the higher authority, and the awaiting congregation is the designated personnel.

What is the purpose of the message being delivered? What does the presenter hope to gain from sharing the message? Where is he headed with the message? When the pilot does not know what port he is heading for, no wind is the right wind; and when the preacher does not know what he is trying to accomplish in his message, no service is a good service. Have a specific aim for each message, and be sure to tell your congregation what it is.

Warren Wiersbe shares the following statements from prominent presenters of the Word of God that relates to the importance of delivery to the message. The following are some of those statements collected and compiled by him:

"A sermon ought to be a monograph and not an encyclopedia," said John Watson, "an agency for pushing one article, not a general store where one can purchase anything from a button to a coffin" (*The Cure of Souls,* p. 18).

If the preacher has done his heart-work and his homework, he should be able to state in one sentence exactly what his message is about and what he wants to accomplish. John Henry Jowett said, "I have a conviction that no sermon is ready for preaching… until we can express its theme in a short, pregnant sentence as clear as crystal" (*The Preacher: His Life and Work,* p. 133).

Teachers of homiletics call this sentence by different terms: the sermon proposition, the theme sentence, the "big idea." This sentence is to the sermon what the spine is to the skeleton, and the foundation to the house: it holds things together and helps to determine what the final product will become.

This proposition should have the following characteristics:

- It should be biblical, a timeless truth that is worth preaching about.

- It should be important and relevant to the needs of the congregation.
- It should be definite and clear, uncluttered by abstract language or literary embellishments.
- It should be accurate and honest and not promise more than the preacher can produce. You don't lay a foundation for a skyscraper and then build a chicken coop on it.
- It should be interesting so that the listener is encouraged to want to listen to the development of the theme in the sermon.
- It should usually be stated in the present tense, what God does for us today and not what he did for Moses centuries ago. "Jesus helped Peter when he was sinking" is a valid statement; but for a sermon thesis, it would better be stated, "In the storms of your life, your Savior is present to help you."

Here are some additional examples:

If you really believe you are going to heaven, then that belief ought to make a difference in your life.

We usually think about the "blessings" of prayer; but have you ever considered prayer as dangerous business?

"The Lord God omnipotent reigneth!" Now, that cardinal conviction will be found, when you explore and examine it, to lead to three results.

—Dr. James S. Stewart

How does the Cross, with its message of forgiveness and healing, affect the memory of sin?

—Dr. William M. Clow

"What think ye of Christ?" Let us go to those who knew Christ, and ask what they thought of Him.

—Dwight L. Moody

What does it do for our prayers to conclude them with the words "through Jesus Christ our Lord"?

—Dr. Ralph W. Sockman

Here, then, are four reasons why people go to church.

—Dr. Leslie D. Weatherhead

Habakkuk, from his vantage point near to the heart of God, gains new insights for the warning of the wicked and the encouragement of the righteous.

—Dr. Charles W. Koller

That brings us to the vital issue. How does faith overcome doubt?

—Dr. Harry Emerson Fosdick" [53]

Since the purpose of proclamation is to meet the human needs of the listeners, the presenter of the Word should be careful how he communicates the Word. He must be careful not to use the proclamation platform to show off his oratorical skills. He must learn to do as John the Baptist, decrease and allow Christ to increase. More of the Master should be manifested in the delivery, and less of the messenger.

There ought to be such simplicity about the message that people will say to themselves, "I could have preached that sermon." Simplicity is a key in delivery. If theological terms are used in the message, be sure you explain them clearly. A simple word is preferred to a technical term, and a concrete word to one that is abstract. Understanding is not born of complexity; it is born of simplicity. The messenger should avoid trying to impress the audience. Preach or teach to express and not impress.

---

[53] Wiersbe, W. W., & Wiersbe, D. 1986. *The elements of preaching: The art of biblical preaching clearly and simply presented.* Tyndale House Publishers: Wheaton, Ill.

Remember, the purpose of preaching is not to stir people to action while bypassing their minds, so that they never see what reason God gives them for doing what the preacher requires of them (that is manipulation); nor is the purpose to stock people's minds with truth that becomes idle and does not become the seedbed and source of changed lives (that is academicism).… The purpose of preaching is to inform, persuade, and call forth an appropriate response to the God whose message and instruction are being delivered.

"Delivering with Passion"

The charge to preach and teach the Word of God should be taken seriously. If the presenter is not serious about sharing the Word of God then he will lack passion in the delivery. God demands and deserves the best delivery of His holy and sacred Word as possible. The messenger should seek to give God his best.

The presenter must determine when he will be negative and when he will be positive as he delivers with passion. Both positive and negative elements are especially effective at accomplishing certain objectives. First let's look at four legitimate reasons to use a negative approach shared by Shelley. "Negative delivery can be used to:

1. *To show our need.* Negative preaching takes sin seriously and leads to repentance, thus indirectly bringing the positive results of joy, peace, and life. It is in keeping with the model of Jesus, who clearly honored God's hatred of sin by telling people what not to do.

In his sermon "God Is an Important Person," John Piper used a negative approach to help listeners see their need to honor God:

I've been to church-growth seminars where God is not once mentioned. I've been to lectures and talks on pastoral issues where he is not so much as alluded to. I have read strategies for every kind of recovery under the sun where God is not there. I have talked to students in seminaries who tell me of manifold courses where God is peripheral at best. I have recently read mission statements of major evangelical organizations where God is not even mentioned.

I admit freely that I'm on a crusade, and I have one message: God is an important person, and he does not like being taken for granted. In this case, the string of negative examples builds forcefully to show listeners their need.

2. ***To seize interest.*** As journalists know—and radio hosts like Rush Limbaugh make a fortune on—the negative gets more attention and interest than the positive.

In his sermon "Power," Howard Hendricks immediately gains a roomful of listeners with an introduction that reminds us our culture is a mess:

Humpty Dumpty sat on a wall.

Humpty Dumpty had a great fall.

All the king's horses and all the king's men

Couldn't put Humpty Dumpty together again.

What a perceptive parable of our generation. We live in a society in which everything nailed down is coming loose. Things that people said could not happen are happening. Thoughtful though unregenerate people are asking, "Where is the glue to reassemble the disintegration and disarray?"

Then we usually seek someone to blame. I saw an intriguing piece of graffiti in the city of Philadelphia some time ago. Scratched across the wall were these words: *Humpty Dumpty was pushed.* After getting listeners' attention with negative news, Hendricks goes on to show that only Christ has the power to straighten out our culture.

3. ***To accentuate the positive.*** The positive feels even
    more so after it has been contrasted with the
    negative.

I appreciated this approach in Leith Anderson's sermon "Can Jesus Trust Us?" Leith develops one point negatively to help us grasp the positive. "Jesus … trusted John with his love. It is a most extraordinary thing to be described as "the one whom Jesus loved," to be Jesus' best friend. It smacks of something inappropriate, but the fact is, that's what their relationship was."

I wonder what it would be like if such a thing were done today…. What would happen if in 1994 someone were identified from all of Christendom as Jesus' best friend? Editors would be lined up for an interview. That person would be on the cover of every magazine. What do you think it would do to that person's life? Do you think that person would write a book or cut a CD or go on the road on a Best-Friend-of-Jesus seminar? Wouldn't it have the high potential of ruining that person's entire life? Wouldn't there be a temptation to arrogance? Wouldn't there be the possibility of treating others in an inappropriate and disparaging way?

And yet, didn't Jesus have as much right to a best friend as any of us? If so, wasn't it critically important that He choose someone whom He could trust to be His best friend, with the confidence that person would never misuse their relationship? By showing the negative way most people would handle such a relationship with Jesus, Leith makes the Apostle John's response seem even more positive.

> 4. **To warn of danger.** If my son reaches toward a hot pan on the stove, it's no time for me to tell him what great potential he has. "Don't touch that pan!" is negative—and necessary. In a dangerous world, much of a responsible pastor's counsel is negative by necessity.

In his sermon "Take Your Best Shot" based on the crucifixion account, Gordon MacDonald uses a negative approach to warn of evils we must avoid. Here are two major forms of evil erupting out of the human experience. One is the crowd's irrational, angry, brutal resistance against God, his purposes and his people. The other is Pilate's saying, "I don't want to be identified with it." In silence and complicity, he backs off, washes his hands, and decides it would be better to do nothing.

What bothers me most is my strong suspicion that I could have been in that crowd.... I can see the possibility of being so defiant against God that I would have joined the crowd saying, "Crucify him!" self-righteously justifying myself. I can also see myself as   Pilate saying, "I don't want anything to do with this," and letting it happen. It's not positive, but it is powerful, and it warns listeners of a danger to avoid." [54]

Shelley shares the following about when to be positive in delivery, "At the core, however, New Testament preachers proclaim good news, a message that brings hope, help, strength, and joy. Jesus sums up the negative commands—don't kill, steal, lie, covet—in positive terms: Love the Lord and love your neighbor.

This positive approach works best when you have the following objectives:

1. ***To show the goodness of Christ.*** The negative often focuses on what people and Satan do. The positive focuses on God's answer, God's glory, God's nature, God's salvation. Christ-centered preaching requires the positive.

In his Easter sermon, "Victory for Us," Earl Palmer shows by an analogy from the Winter Olympics that Christ won a victory not only for Himself, but also for us:

---

[54] Shelley, M. 1995. *Changing lives through preaching and worship : 30 strategies for powerful communication.* "Was previously published in Leadership, by Christianity Today, Inc."--T.p. verso. (1st ed.). Library of Christian leadership, Moorings: Nashville, Tenn.

147

"The high point of the Olympics from a sentimental standpoint is those award ceremonies. When the victors stand on those three pedestals, that's where everybody is crying. The three flags are raised, and the national anthem of the gold medalist is played.

Something else is signified there: not only did [the various skaters] win, but their countries won, too. Not only their countries but their parents. Notice how the cameras try to find parents in the audience and the skaters' trainers and sometimes a whole town in Wisconsin—they all share in that victory. That's what makes it great. They not only won for themselves, they won for us, too."

In the Easter narratives of the New Testament, two great affirmations are made. One affirmation is that Christ has won the victory, and it's His alone. But the second theme, perhaps more subtly portrayed but also present in all the Gospel narratives, is that we too win a victory on Easter day. Our Lord's victory is His vindication, but it's also our vindication. The positive approach fits the theme of resurrection and life.

2. *To bring encouragement and hope.* God wants people to experience hope, peace, acceptance, courage. Bad news makes people feel bad. So while the negative is useful, it is rarely helpful to leave that as the last word.

148

In his sermon "Listening to the Dark," Eugene Lowry comforts listeners from the story of God speaking in a still, small voice to the despairing Elijah: In the midst of the darkness of the cave finally came this voice. The voice came up close to the ear and whispered. And the voice said, "What are you doing here?"

That's one of the most remarkable passages in all of Scripture. What do you mean, "What are you doing *here*?" Do you notice what the voice did not say? It did not say "What are you doing *there*?"—as though God were distant and aloof, looking on to the scene of the cave saying, "What are you doing there, Elijah? Why are you there?" We're not talking *there*, we're talking *here*.

God is in the dark. In fact, God is bigger than the dark. That's the promise. It is God's dark. God is the Creator of the dark. And the promise is that God will be present…. And so with the confidence of children of the Most High God, revealed in Christ, we may dare to endure the dark.

3. *To build godliness.* People need not only to stop sinning, but also to start doing God's will. Preaching is both destructive and constructive, tearing down what's wrong and building what's right. Preaching positively encourages people to do what's right.

In his sermon "No Ordinary People," Wayne Brouwer affirms the right things the people in his congregation are doing:

One of the great privileges we have as pastors is to hear the things that people say to us when they first join us for worship and for fellowship. Seven times this past week alone, I've heard things like this:

"I didn't know what Christianity was about until I came to First Church."

"You people at First Church made me feel welcome even when I didn't know what I needed in my own soul."

"You know," said one person, "I dropped out of church for many years. I didn't think I needed it. And then my friend brought me to First Church one day. Now I know what I've been missing. I'd like to become a member."

"People at First Church really live their faith, don't they?"

That's what they're saying about us. They're not really saying it about us. They're saying it about Christ in us.

This positive approach surely made Brouwer's congregation want to continue to accept newcomers.

4. ***To bring resolution.*** Sermons often have greater emotional impact when we begin with the negative, show the need, and then bring resolution by showing what God can do.

In his sermon "The Love That Compels," Stuart Briscoe shows the classic negative-to-positive form of Christian preaching: the sin of humanity and the salvation of Christ.

Human beings are not unlike volcanoes. Inside a volcano, the pressure builds until the top blows with a dramatic eruption of lava. At other times, cracks slowly and insidiously appear on the side of the volcano, and the lava flows out in a different manner....

Inside each of us, there's a thing called *sin.* No matter what way our volcano was formed, whether we blow the top or leak streams of lava, it's the lava inside that's the problem. The ultimate disease is the problem, and there's nothing human beings can do about it.

God demonstrated his incredible love toward us when he took the initiative and determined to do something about the sin problem. He invited Christ to take our sins on himself and die our deaths. God would no longer count our sins against us. He would reckon the sin to Christ and reckon to us the righteousness of Christ. That's love. Notice that the negative opening doesn't find resolution until the positive conclusion." [55]

Shelley also offers suggestions about changing directions between the negative and the positive. "As we ponder the purpose of our sermon, we may sense that we need to flip an element from positive to negative, or vice versa. Instead of saying what not to do, we want to focus on what to do. Or instead of illustrating what someone did right, we want to illustrate what someone did wrong. Here's how to make the switch.

1. *Switching from negative to positive.* In a sermon on James 1:24, I wanted to encourage listeners to persevere because it makes them mature in character. I suspected, though, that many of my listeners weren't overly concerned about growing in character. But I also assumed they don't want to crash and burn morally. So I began by using a

---

[55] Shelley, M. 1995. *Changing lives through preaching and worship: 30 strategies for powerful communication.* "Was previously published in Leadership, by Christianity Today, Inc."--T.p. verso. (1st ed.). Library of Christian leadership. Moorings: Nashville, Tenn.

negative example, trying to motivate them by showing them what to avoid:

No one wants to crash and burn.

On September 8, 1992, United States Air Force master pilot Don Snelgrove was flying over Turkey in an F-16 fighter. He was on a four-hour mission to patrol the no-flight zone established over northern Iraq to protect the Kurds.

Nature calls even for master pilots. He pulled out a plastic container, set his F-16 on autopilot, and undid his lap belt. As he adjusted his seat upward, the buckle on that lap belt wedged between the seat and the control stick, pushing the stick to the right and sending the plane into a spin.

As he struggled to regain control, the plane plunged 33,000 feet. Finally at 2,000 feet altitude, he ejected from the plane. Moments later the F-16 struck a barren hillside and burst into flames. Neither the pilot nor anyone on the ground was injured. But I'll tell you what: there was one very embarrassed master pilot. That F-16 burning on a hillside in Turkey cost U.S. taxpayers 18 million dollars.

Even inadvertent mistakes are terribly embarrassing. How much worse are the mistakes and failures that result from our weaknesses, flaws, and sins. But we don't have to crash and burn morally. We can develop godly character, and James 1:24 shows us how.

My goal was to use negative examples to motivate. But I could have begun the sermon positively. Perhaps the congregation already desired character and needed only encouragement. In that case, I could have begun the sermon with a positive example of someone who inspires us with his or her noble character:

Inside each of us there is the desire to be a better person. Many of us would love to be more like Dr. Elizabeth Holland, a pediatrician from Memphis, Tennessee, who has served as a volunteer doctor for World Vision.

Once she treated patients in the middle of an African civil war, says writer Robert Kerr. In 1985 she performed one appendectomy in which "the 'operating room' was a mud hut deep in the jungle of Zaire. The anesthetic was an animal tranquilizer, which ran out in the middle of the operation. Outside, MIG jets were dropping bombs." Every time a bomb hit, dirt from the mud hut fell down on them. She performed a virtual miracle considering the circumstances, and her patient lived.

During the Angolan civil war, Holland routinely saw 400 to 500 patients a day. "'I frequently wrapped broken bones in magazines and used banana leaves for slings,' she said."

Since food was in short supply, Holland ate a paste made from ground cassava-plant roots. "It tasted like glue," said Dr. Holland. "The first few days, I thought I would die. But then I got to where it tasted pretty good. Sometimes when it rained we could get a few leaves from the trees to cook in with it for variety."

Across the Angolan border was a minefield that often killed or injured civilians; Holland would retrieve them. "She said, 'I learned if I got my nose down at ground level and crawled along on my stomach, I could see the mines. So I would make my way across, then throw the injured person over my shoulder and carry them out the same way I had come over.'"

Maybe we will never be forced to persevere as Elizabeth Holland has, but each of us can grow in character, and James 1:24 tell us how.

Notice that this example leaves a positive feeling in listeners; it assumes they want the best and can develop. The negative approach focuses on what to avoid; a positive approach focuses on what to attempt.

2. *Switching from positive to negative.* Familiar Bible passages can be presented in a positive or negative approach, depending upon the situation. Take, for example, the story of Peter trying to walk on water.

In his sermon "A Mind-Expanding Faith," John Ortberg drew from the text a positive main idea:

All of us are "would-be water walkers." And God did not intend for human beings, his children created in his divine image, to go through life in a desperate attempt to avoid failure.

The boat is safe, and the boat is secure, and the boat is comfortable. The water is high, the waves are rough, the wind is strong, and the night is dark. A storm is out there, and if you get out of your boat, you may sink.

But if you don't get out of your boat, you will never walk because if you want to walk on the water, you have to get out of the boat. There is something, Someone, inside us that tells us our lives are about something more than sitting in the boat, something that wants to walk on the water, something that calls us to leave the routine of comfortable existence and abandon ourselves in this adventure of following Christ.

But the same passage could be used in a negative approach: to point out Peter's mistakes to avoid. It might sound like this:

Peter was able to walk on water for a few steps. But in the middle of that walk toward Christ, something changed in his heart, and it caused him to sink.

Peter isn't the only one who has taken bold steps of faith to follow Christ. Many in this congregation are doing the same. In spite of great fear, you have begun to teach a Bible class or host a cell group or volunteer at the local hospital. Now that you've begun, you are beginning to see how challenging this really is, and you're wavering. You feel like you're going to sink. Let's see if we can learn from this account how to avoid what caused Peter to sink. To change from positive to negative, look for what a text shows not to do." [56]

---

[56] Shelley, M. 1995. *Changing lives through preaching and worship : 30 strategies for powerful communication.* "Was previously published in

When communicating the Word, the presenter must remember that no two preachers/teachers are the same. The passion one has for the Word may be presented differently than the other; however, both should have their own. The human personality is a vital part of the proclamation ministry and it should be expressed. The presenter must be careful not to imitate the personality of anyone else and just release his own God-given personality in the delivery.

"God prepares the person who prepares the message. Martin Luther said that prayer, meditation, and temptation made a preacher. Prayer and meditation will give you a sermon, but only temptation—the daily experience of life—can transform that sermon into a message. It's the difference between the recipe and the meal." [57]

"Abraham Lincoln said, "When I hear a man preach, I like to see him act as if he were fighting bees." Exuberance has its attractions, but zealous preaching also packs liabilities. Flailing limbs may so dominate the pulpit that the preacher's zeal upstages the sermon's intent.

Leadership, by Christianity Today, Inc."--T.p. verso. (1st ed.). Library of Christian leadership . Moorings: Nashville, Tenn.
[57] Shelley, M. 1995.

On the other hand, pastors able to weave a literate spell with smooth oratory want to do more than impress a receptive crowd. The art of preaching is not intended to displace the aim: hearts moved to believe in Christ and follow his ways.

According to Calvin Miller, combining zeal, art, and results is no recent quandary. Even Old Testament prophets faced the dilemma. Miller, pastor of Westside Baptist Church in Omaha and a popular author, strives to make both art and zeal serve his preaching and writing purposes." [58]

"Phillips Brooks defined preaching as "the bringing of truth through personality" (*Lectures on Preaching,* p. 5). The preacher is not only a herald, but also a witness. He has personally experienced the power of God's truth in his own life and therefore can share it with others.

The incarnation of Christ is evidence that God mediates his truth through human personality. "And the Word was made flesh and dwelt among us…." (John 1:14). As the preacher grows, so grows the message, and so grows the church. It is not enough to have the authority of the Word behind the sermon; one must also evidence the power of a life lived under the authority of that Word.

---

[58] Berkley, J. D. 1986. *Vol. 8: Preaching to convince.* "A Leadership/Word book"--T.p. verso. The Leadership library. CTI; Word Books: Carol Stream, Ill.; Waco, TX

This explains why the preacher suffers: God is teaching him new lessons of faith for the encouragement of his people. It also explains why the preacher must cultivate his own personal walk with the Lord. The pulpit is no place for borrowed blessings. They must flow out of the minister's fellowship with God in order to be fresh and exciting.

In other words, the preacher as well as the sermon must be prepared. The two go together. In every part of his being— physical, mental, emotional, spiritual—the preacher must be a prepared vessel to contain, and then to share, the message of life. What God has joined together, let not preachers put asunder." [59]

Although the preacher/teacher is a vital partner in the message, he should be careful not to become the focus of the message. He must guard himself especially when he speaks of his personal experiences with God not to exalt self instead of the Savior. This does not mean that he shouldn't share his personal feelings and experiences. He should share what Christ has done in his life but he should always remember that he has a charge to preach Christ, and Him crucified.

---

[59] Wiersbe, W. W., & Wiersbe, D. 1986. *The elements of preaching: The art of biblical preaching clearly and simply presented.* Tyndale House Publishers: Wheaton, Ill.

Some presenters of the Word are guilty of talking about themselves too much. Others are so private that their personal experiences are told as anonymous anecdotes. Both extremes should be avoided. The congregation wants to see Christ, but they want to see Him through the ministry of a real person, even one who occasionally makes mistakes.

In his book *Preaching and Preachers* Martyn Lloyd-Jones recounts an event from his first year of preaching that relates to delivery of the message. This is what he had to say: "It was the custom in Wales at that time, on special occasions, to have two preachers who preached together in a service, the younger man first and the older one following.... The old man was kind enough to listen to me in the afternoon, and it was the first time he had heard me trying to preach. As we were being driven in a car together to have some tea at the house of the minister of the church, the old preacher, who was exactly sixty years older than I was, very kindly and with a desire to help and to encourage me gave me a very serious warning. "The great defect of that sermon this afternoon was this," he said, "that you were overtaxing your people, you were giving them too much.... You are only stunning them, and therefore you are not helping them." And then he said, "You watch what I shall be doing tonight. I shall really be saying one thing, but I shall say it in three different ways." And that was precisely what he did, and most effectively."[60]

The presenter should seek to avoid complex outlines and complex dialogue that will cause the listeners to miss the message. I use repetition to help the listener capture the main emphasis of the message and try to smoothly move from one point to the next with a transitional statement. For example, if my first point in the message is "the favor of the Lord", then I will move from point one to point two by making the similar transitional statement " not only does Paul share with us about the favor of the Lord, but he also shares with us about his faith in the Lord." I use these transitional statements throughout the message so the listener can keep up with the flow of the message. My outline of the message is also printed in the church bulletin with space for note taking to help in this process.

G. Campbell Morgan argues that "*passion* is an essential ingredient for an effective delivery." In explaining what he means by "passion," he recalls a discussion the English actor Macready had with a well-known pastor. The pastor was trying to understand why crowds flocked to fictional plays but few came to hear him preach God's changeless truth. Macready responded, "This is quite

---

[60] D. Martyn Lloyd-Jones, *Preaching and Preachers* (Grand Rapids: Zondervan, 1971), 257.

simple.... I present my fiction as though it were truth; you present your truth as though it were fiction." [61]

Morgan also states, "I am not arguing for mere excitement. Painted fire never burns, and an imitated enthusiasm is the most empty thing that can possibly exist in a preacher. Given the preacher with a message ..., I cannot understand that man not being swept sometimes right out of himself by the fire and the force and the fervency of his work." [62]

Kaiser defines passion by stating "from the beginning of the sermon to its end, the all engrossing force of the text and the God who speaks through that text must dominate our whole being. With the burning power of that truth on our heart and lips, every thought, emotion, and act of the will must be so captured by that truth that it springs forth with excitement, joy, sincerity, and reality as an evident token that God's Spirit is in that word. Away with all the mediocre, lifeless, boring, and lackluster orations offered as pitiful substitutes for the powerful Word of the living Lord. If that Word from God does not thrill the proclaimer and fill [him] ...

---

[61] D. Martyn Lloyd-Jones, *Preaching and Preachers* (Grand Rapids: Zondervan, 1971), 257.

[62] Ibid., 37.

163

with an intense desire to glorify God and do His will, how shall we ever expect it to have any greater effect on our hearers?" [63]

"Delivering with Power"

Hebrews 4:12 states "For the word of God is quick and powerful, and sharper than any two-edged sword, piercing even to the dividing asunder of soul and spirit, and the joints and marrow, and is a discerner of the thoughts and intents of the heart." [64] The Bible teaches that there is power in the Word of God. His Word is alive. Since it is alive, it should be delivered with power. How can this happen? There are several ways.

To deliver with power is to deliver with the aid of the *Comforter.* The presenter should acknowledge his total dependence on the Holy Spirit to empower and energize him as he yields himself as a vessel to the service of the Lord. Proclamation without recognizing and relying on the power of the Holy Spirit is vain.

To deliver with power is also to deliver with *confidence.* If you believe that what you have to say is true, then you should say it with assurance and authority. A message delivered without

---

[63] Walter C. Kaiser, *Toward An Exegetical Theology* (Grand Rapids: Baker, 1981), 239.
[64] *The Holy Bible: King James Version*

confidence is often a message delivered without yielding change in the hearts of the listeners.

The message should also be delivered with *celebration*. Why should the congregation get excited about what you have to say when you're not excited? The Prophet Jeremiah described the message God gave him to deliver as "fire shut up in his bones." The Word of God should be released in such a manner that the congregation should see the excitement in you and the flame will kindle their excitement. The presenter should step to the platform with his cup running over with the excitement of the joy of the Lord.

The message should be delivered with celebration because proclaiming the Word is an act of worship. Wiersbe shares, "If it is not, then it will call attention to itself or to the preacher, and not to God. When preaching is not an act of worship, there is the danger that the congregation may worship the preacher and not God.

When a man has a high view of preaching, he will reach higher in his preaching. Paul looked upon his ministry as that of a priest at the altar: "… be a minister of Christ Jesus to the Gentiles, ministering the gospel of God, that the offering up of the Gentiles might be acceptable, being sanctified by the Holy Spirit" (Rom. 15:16).

If our preaching is an act of worship, we will want to give God our best. We will also seek to honor Him, not glorify ourselves or try to show people how learned or clever we are. Furthermore, the sermon will then fit into the total context of worship so that everything in the service will point to the Savior.

"You can never make a sermon what it ought to be," said Phillips Brooks, "if you consider it alone. The service that accompanies it, the prayer and praise, must have their influence upon it" (*op. cit.*, p. 142)." [65]

The following is a pattern I use to ensure that on the Lord's Day I will deliver the best presentation possible:

1. Thursday is my prayer and preparation day for the sermon. I make it a practice to try to have my rough draft completed on Thursday afternoon. This consists of research notes, an exegesis of the passage, and the message outline. Since I'm not a manuscript preacher, there is no written message. Most messengers preach and teach from a manuscript, however, I prefer the freedom of the outline. By Thursday evening, all research material is ready for the pulling together of the passage to be presented.

---

[65] Wiersbe, W. W., & Wiersbe, D. 1986. *The elements of preaching: The art of biblical preaching clearly and simply presented.* Tyndale House Publishers: Wheaton, Ill.

2. On Friday morning, I put the final touches on the message and about noon I enter into relaxation and prepare for Friday family night with my wife and daughter.

3. On Saturday morning, I return to the office for a few hours and go over the message to become intimately familiar with it. Saturday night before I go to bed, I review my study notes and try to go to bed with the message on my mind. Many times I find myself preaching through and praying for the message in my sleep.

4. On Sunday morning, as I enter the office, I try not to handle any business before I enter the sanctuary to begin preaching the Word. I want to be totally focused on the assignment at hand, proclaiming the Word of God to the people of God.

The following are frequently asked questions and answers concerning the proclamation ministry that may yield helpful in effective delivery:

How long does it take you to prepare a message?

I spend about eight to ten hours in the preparatory process. I used to spend more time but the availability of good resources has shortened the preparation.

How do you guard your preparation time for Sunday's message?

Thursday has been designated as my message preparation and prayer day for Sunday's message. My administrative assistant helps to shield my time by screening all my calls and making sure that I am not disturbed on that day unless desperately needed. Only when I have accomplished what I need to on that day do I then stop and care for other matters. I continue this process on Friday morning. Saturday morning is more flexible. I mix family time and study time and will usually close the night with review time so I can rest with the message on my mind.

Whenever there are other responsibilities that may call for me to deviate from my scheduled study time, I put in overtime to make sure that sufficient time is spent with the Author and the Book, God and the Bible.

To what extent do you use notes? Do you write a manuscript?

Once I have collected my research material and formed my outline to the message, I then put things in a flowing order from the rough draft. I fill in the outline points and sub-points with information. This information is what I will share on Sunday from memory with the aid of the Holy Spirit. When I enter the pulpit, I enter with only a Bible. My outline is printed in the bulletin for the membership and I have one in the pulpit for my use as well.

This is my method and the one I have become accustomed to. I have discovered from talking to manuscript preachers and teachers that they write out notes from the manuscript to take into the pulpit: these aids consist of about ten half-sheets of notes for each message. They write out everything they desire to cover and some statements are written exactly the way they desire to phrase them.

MacArthur shares this concerning manuscript preaching: "Since I preach in the same church week after week, I do not want to phrase the same truths in exactly the same way time after time. To keep my messages new, I need to guard against falling back into habitual ways of saying things. Extensive notes help me avoid that. They also assure that I do not forget something important I wanted to say. Since I use many cross-references, I need to write down their chapter and verse as well.

My notes are the record of my study of a passage, so I try to make them thorough. If they are too cryptic, I will not remember my flow of thought later when I review them. For example, if my notes say, "Tell story of boy and dog," six months later I may not remember what boy and what dog. Even referring to an Old Testament story requires some notes, so I can recall later what nuance of that story was relevant. I am also writing a commentary series on the entire New Testament. Sometimes the commentary on a book is written several years after I have preached through the book. My notes need to have enough of my exegesis to reflect how I interpreted a passage for the sake of this later use.

I am not really bound to my notes when I preach. I do not read a manuscript. On Saturday evening (or Sunday afternoon for the Sunday-evening message) I read through my notes and highlight key points with a red pen. These red notations are a visual crutch if I need them. I have learned through experience how to look at my notes while I am preaching without it being obvious to the congregation. I could preach my sermons without my notes. I might forget a few things, or not say something exactly the way I wanted to, but the main thrust of my message would be there." [66]

What use do you make of quotes and illustrations?

Quotes and illustrations are very helpful in getting and keeping the attention of the listener. I try to credit the individual that I am quoting because it seems to give more validity to what is being expressed. It is also important to keep in mind that the Scripture is authoritative and does not need outside support.

---

[66] MacArthur, J. 1997, c1992. *Rediscovering expository preaching.* Word Pub.: Dallas

Regardless of what someone else has to say about the Scripture, it doesn't add to It being right. It is the truth with or without any other support.

Giving credit to the quote or illustration should be done but sometimes it may be difficult. Macarthur writes, "Yet I read so many different discussions and pour so many things through my mind as I prepare my sermons that it is next to impossible to document the source of each thought. As long as I phrase the thoughts in my own words and combine them with other thoughts, it is not necessary to footnote them. Extensive footnoting is proper in a book. I am careful in my books to document my sources, but too many references to sources would be distracting in a sermon.

A balance is the ideal. We cannot document every thought in our sermons. On the other hand, we should give credit where due. Pastors sometimes ask me if they can use my material. I have given blanket permission for anyone to use my sermons and preach them in whole or in part if they wish, and I do not want any credit as the source. If what I say has value to someone, I am honored for him to use it for God's glory. The truth is all His.

Yet if someone re-preaches one of my sermons without enriching it by going through the discovery process, that sermon will inevitably be flat and lifeless. The great Scottish preacher Alexander Maclaren once went to hear another man preach, a young man with a reputation for being a gifted preacher. Much to Maclaren's surprise, the young man said at the outset of his message, "I've had such a busy week that I had no time to prepare a sermon of my own, so I'm going to preach one of Maclaren's." He did not know Maclaren was in the audience until Maclaren greeted him afterward. He was very embarrassed and became even more so when Maclaren looked him in the eye and said, "Young man, I don't mind if you are going to preach my sermons, but if you are going to preach them like that, please don't say they are mine."

To rely too heavily on the sermons of others robs one of the joy of discovering biblical truth for himself. Such sermons will lack conviction and enthusiasm. Sermons by other preachers should be another study tool, like commentaries or illustration books." [67]

Do you practice your sermons before you deliver them on Sunday?

I wouldn't refer to what I do when I'm meditating on the delivery of the message as practice. I believe that no dress rehearsal will prepare you for the real event that will take place on Sunday morning. I do find myself preaching the message to

[67] MacArthur, J. 1997, c1992. *Rediscovering Expository Preaching.* Word Pub.: Dallas

myself during the course of the day, while I'm meditating, or during my personal workout times and even on Saturday night when I'm preparing for sleep. There are some Sunday mornings when I arise remembering that I preached the message in my sleep.

How long should a message be?

The message should be long enough to say what you have to say and short enough for the people to listen to what you have to say. The messenger should be conscious of time but he must make sure that he doesn't rush and mishandle the Word of God. He should adequately cover the passage. I usually preach for about thirty minutes. The important thing is to take the necessary time to effectively cover the material that God has given you to share with His people.

My goal as it relates to the time of the message is to close the door on the message in thirty minutes. I use about four minutes to introduce the message, twenty-three minutes for the body of the message, and about three minutes to close the message. More time should always be given to biblical exposition than to the introduction or closing. There are many presenters of the Word that place more emphasis on the introduction and especially the closing of the message than the body. We must keep the main thing the main thing. The body is the main thing.

Developing an outline and being committed to the outline will help the presenter as well as the people to stay focused and to follow the logical flow of the message. The message will always work better when the presenter knows where he is going and when the people can clearly see how to follow. If the message lacks a logical flow because it is disjointed, the people will lose interest and begin to follow something else. Their minds will wander into other areas of interest.

As it relates to time, remember, the purpose for making the presentation of the Word is not to get over, but rather to explain the Word of God.

Do people get tired of series preaching or teaching?

Series preaching/teaching is a great method for sharing the Word. It has several advantages. First, the messenger will know exactly what he needs to cover and what he will be covering in the upcoming weeks. This will eliminate wasting a lot of time trying to figure out what to preach. The agenda has been preset. It also helps the audience to keep up with the direction that the minister is leading the church, and many will feel that they have missed something special if they miss a message.

When preaching/teaching through a series that is three or more months long, it is good to give the congregation a break periodically; unless the series is through one of the Gospels, such may not be necessary. The reason being is that the Gospels contain such a mixture of doctrinal passages, parables, and narrative passages that they change tempo often on their own.

Why do you use expository preaching?

Expository preaching means unfolding the text of Scripture in a way that makes contact with the listeners' world while exalting Christ and confronting them with the need for action. I believe that preaching verse by verse through the Bible is the best process for presenting the purity of the passage. To fail to practice expository preaching is not a matter to be taken lightly. There are costly consequences:

1. *Misunderstanding.* When Paul wrote to Titus he warned him (and us) about the "many unruly and vain talkers and deceivers…whose mouths must be stopped" (Titus 1:10-11). This is clearly the responsibility of the elders. How are they to accomplish this? By a thorough knowledge of the Scriptures and the Gospel. An elder "must hold firmly to the trustworthy message as it has been taught, so that he can encourage others by sound doctrine and refute those who oppose it" (v. 9).

It is the work of the Word to teach, rebuke, correct, and train so that God's people can set out on the voyage of life

175

equipped for search and rescue. When the Bible is not being systematically expounded, congregations often learn a little about a lot but usually do not understand how everything fits together. They are like workers in a car assembly plant who know how to add their particular component but remain largely clueless as to how it fits in with the rest of the process. The most dangerous people in our churches are those who are susceptible to all kinds of passing fads and fancies; they often prove to be a trial to themselves as well as to others.

It is striking that in a time of great moral and doctrinal confusion, Paul exhorted Timothy not to spend his time learning clever answers to silly questions, but rather to give his time and energy to preaching the Word of God (2 Tim. 4:2-5).

2. *Malnutrition*. As Walter C. Kaiser has written, "It is no secret that Christ's Church is not in good health in many places of the world. She has been languishing because she has been fed, as the current line has it, "junk food"; all kinds of artificial preservatives and all sorts of unnatural substitutes have been served up to her. As a result, theological and biblical malnutrition has afflicted the very generation that has taken such giant steps to make sure its physical health is not damaged by using foods or products that are harmful to their bodies. Simultaneously a worldwide spiritual famine resulting from the absence of any

genuine publication of the Word of God (Amos 8:11) continues to run wild and almost unabated in most quarters of the Church." [68]

Hebrews 5:12-13 describes those who are stunted in their growth as a result of being stuck on "baby food." Because of the neglect of proper nourishment, their spiritual appetites became spoiled, the power of digestion became lacking, and they were brought back to a state of second childhood. A lack of proper feeding and feasting on the Word will cause this in the life of any individual. Expository preaching is the cure.

Expository preaching has a number of advantages over topical preaching. First of all, its *points* of application are more compelling because the hearers see that the application legitimately emerges from the Bible. Secondly, it *portrays* to Christians how to study and interpret the Bible for themselves. Thirdly, it *presents* confidence not in the persuasiveness of the preacher, but in the power of God's Word to change people.

Expository preaching challenges the student of the Word to present the complete counsel of God. Being committed to preaching and teaching the whole counsel of God can only be done by examining and expounding one verse at a time throughout the entire Bible. This commitment to sharing the Word of God

---

[68] *Toward an Exegetical Theology* [Grand Rapids, Mich: Baker, 1981], pp. 7-8.

systematically, so that all of the revelation of God is brought before His people, is the only effective way of keeping Scripture in its context.

A verse by verse study of the Word sets the passage in its context on its *widest*, *warmest*, and *wealthiest* level. Please note that neither the Old Testament nor the New Testament was written as an anthology of verses to stand by itself, but rather as a whole letter to be communicated together.

Where does storytelling fit into expository preaching?

One of the greatest storytellers I have encountered in the preaching ministry is the Reverend Jerry Black, pastor of the Beulah Baptist Church in Decatur, Georgia. He has been blessed with the ability to paint a vivid picture as he presents the passage. Although I often use simple analogies throughout the message, I don't consider myself a storyteller. I use analogies to pull up the shades so somebody can see a teaching more clearly.

The presenter of the passage must understand that stories, although they have great emotional impact, is no comparison with the power of the Scripture. MacArthur writes about stories, "People respond to a story with the idea, "Now I can sit back and hear this nice story. I call it communication in the light vein. I would rather find a concise analogy or an Old Testament illustration and keep the sermon moving than get caught in some long story that might send the wrong signal to people. I want them to stay at my level of intensity. When I think they need a few relaxing moments, I will break in with a breather such as a funny statement or something that is simple. I try to pace the message that way. In my mind, stories tend to shut down the level of intensity that I prefer people to maintain. I tell a story when it is appropriate, but this happens only rarely. I like to think that I can say the same thing as effectively with a brief comparison."[69]

I've heard it said that 50 percent of a message should be application. Could you comment?

Application should be one of the main reasons for presenting the message. I believe the goal of preaching is to challenge and compel people to make a decision. After they have heard God's Word, then a decision needs to be made to say either, "Yes, I will do what God says," or "No, I won't do what God says." This is application.

While I believe in the importance of illustrations, I do not believe that 50 percent of a sermon must be applications. The presenter must be conscious of the fact that it is the Spirit who applies the shared truths of the Scripture to each person through

---

[69] MacArthur, J. 1997, c1992. *Rediscovering Expository Preaching.* Word Pub.: Dallas

the principles given to be applied. Failure to present the listener with principles leaves him with nothing to apply.

Do you ever get nervous when you preach?

I must admit when I first started preaching that nervousness was one of my struggles; however, the more opportunities I had to share the Word publicly the more comfortable I became with the presentation. I am never nervous when it comes to the material I am sharing because I am always prepared. If the presenter is unprepared or unfamiliar with the message then he would have a reason to be nervous. The best defense against nervousness is preparation.

John Macarthur was asked the following questions about sermon delivery and he provided this commentary based on his many years of experience from serving as pastor and from preaching the Word of God:

"How do you find the balance between instructing people and playing to their emotions?

Emotions are important. They were given to us by God, and they often move the will. People do not usually make decisions in an emotional vacuum. I do want to stir people's emotions when I preach, because truth that warms the heart can move the will.

When Jesus spoke of true worship, He described it as worship "in spirit and truth" (John 4:23–24). What He meant was that emotion and truth in combination constitute true worship. Our worship of God must be based on truth, yet should also involve the emotions. It should be our goal to encourage the proper components in worship. The hymns and special music, as well as the pastoral prayer and sermon, must articulate truth. Yet they should also stir the emotions and activate the will.

What I oppose is artificially stimulating the emotions in isolation or separation from truth. This practice smacks of manipulation and peddling the Word of God (cf. 2 Cor. 2:17). Two extremes must be avoided: truth without emotions and emotions without truth. The two are seen in Jesus' discussion with the Samaritan woman in John 4. The Samaritans' worship was enthusiastic and emotional, but not based on truth. On the other hand, the Jews' worship was based on truth, but was cold, unemotional, and dead. Both were wrong. True worship is based on truth, and involves the emotions.

How do you differentiate between persuasion and manipulation?

The difference lies in the means we use to persuade. The Word of God is the only legitimate means of persuasion.

Legitimate persuasion is cognitive—stirring the mind with reasonable truth. Convincing with tear-jerking stories, histrionics, and emotional outbursts takes an unfair advantage of people and wrongly muddles their thinking. That does not mean we cannot use all the communication skills available to us, but we should avoid playing on people's emotions, even by repeated singing or playing of hymns. These are artificial and should be avoided because they bypass the reason.

Our goal in preaching is to constrain people to choose change because it is reasonable and right before God, not because they have been manipulated into some momentary feeling or action. We persuade them from the Scriptures to choose the right course of action. We do not pile on emotional pressure until they break. We want them to know clearly what the alternatives are and that they must choose. If after hearing our sermon someone does not know what he is supposed to do about it, we did not reach that person. I believe the legitimate point of persuasion ends with the clear presentation of the truth and must not move beyond that to artificial emotional stimuli for eliciting a response. This latter kind of appeal has produced false Christians and weak believers bouncing from one emotional high to another without a theology to live by.

In 1 Tim. 4:13, Paul writes to Timothy, "Till I come, give attendance to reading, to exhortation, to doctrine." What he tells Timothy is to read the text, explain the text, and apply the text. That verse is a call to persuasive, expository preaching. Paul himself was a very persuasive preacher, but he never tried to manipulate emotions to move people artificially. At the end of one of his messages, King Agrippa exclaimed, "Almost thou persuadest me to be a Christian" (Acts 26:28). Agrippa clearly understood the message. Unfortunately, he made a wrong decision in spite of his understanding.

Ultimately, however, our sermons will only be as persuasive as our lives. A traveling speaker who does not remain in one place long enough for people to get to know him may be able to "fake" it without a consistent life to back up his message, (though this is regrettable). Those of us who preach to the same people week after week, however, cannot do that. Our people know us, and our persuasiveness depends on the quality of our lives. Paul's preaching was persuasive; but it was his *life* that won the hearts of people. The Ephesian elders cried when Paul left them, but not because they would not hear him preach anymore. They were "grieving especially over the word which he had spoken, that they should see his face no more" (Acts 20:38). The integrity of the preacher's life is a key element in persuasiveness.

What are your thoughts on drama in the pulpit?

I was at a pastors' conference where one of the speakers came out in diapers with a doll under one arm, a pacifier around his neck, and a baby bottle in his hand. He proceeded to talk about baby Christians. In my judgment I would have to say that such a performance appears to be a crutch; and it seems that only a weak preacher would need such a crutch. You have to believe that the power of God's Word will be more effective than any human drama or communication gimmick. Nothing is as dramatic as the explosion of truth on the mind of a believer through powerful preaching.

How do you get yourself up for a sermon when you've been down during the week?

I often work harder on my sermons when I am not doing so well. Feeling good and excited about my message tends to carry me. When I feel bad, which is very rare, I know I have to give it everything I have, and I turn up the effort. It is similar to athletics. Many athletes exert themselves more when they feel below par.

The same is true when I think my message is not too exciting. I work harder to find ways to make it exciting. Often those sermons turn out to be better than others in which the material is great.

Do you have an illustration file?

If I find a good illustration, I usually use it right away. I do have a file, but in the years I have been in the ministry, it has grown large and cumbersome. So much material is in it that it is tedious and time-consuming to go through it. Keeping track of illustrations is one area where a personal computer is of immense help.

Do you use a preaching calendar to schedule your messages?

I have a general plan in that, before I finish the books I am currently preaching from, I decide what books I want to preach through next. But I cannot schedule what to cover week by week. As I mentioned earlier, I do not always know what I will cover until I begin preaching. This makes preaching an adventure, but it also means a preaching calendar would have to be revised so frequently that it would be useless.

Since I generally preach through books of the New Testament, a preaching calendar for me is unnecessary. I know what passage I will be preaching each Sunday. A preaching calendar is useful for those who preach topically. Wasting precious study time each week trying to figure out what to preach on should be avoided.

Even when I re-preach an old set of expositions, I cannot set a fixed schedule because I may encounter a theme that takes more time than I planned.

What two or three books on preaching have profoundly impacted your thinking?

The first book that affected my thinking was John Broadus's *on The Preparation and Delivery of Sermons.* A second book that really hit me hard was John Stott's book *The Preacher's Portrait* in which he explained five New Testament words that pictured the preacher's vast responsibility and duty. Then I read D. Martyn Lloyd-Jones's *Preachers and Preaching.* Those three have influenced me greatly.

What abiding lessons would you teach men who are committed to expository preaching that will sustain them for a lifetime of ministry?

First of all, make sure that every expository message has a single theme that is crystal clear so that your people know exactly what you are saying, how you have supported it, and how it is to be applied to their lives. The thing that kills people is that what is sometimes called expository preaching is randomly meandering through a passage. Secondly, when you go into a church that is not

186

accustomed to exposition, realize that a period of training the listeners is needed. You must move your flock from whatever they have been hearing into thinking logically, rationally, and even deeply about the Word of God. This is the process of weaning them from whatever they have been on and whetting their appetites for the meat of God's Word.

Next, you need to go in with a long-term perspective. My dad said to me years ago, "I want you to remember a couple of things before you go into the ministry. One, the great preachers, the lasting preachers who left their mark on history, taught their people the Word of God. Two, they stayed in one place for a long time." These were two good pieces of advice. Everybody used to say, when I first came to Grace Community Church, that I would only last about a year or two, because they saw me as a communicator. But in my heart, I knew I wanted to do two things: one was to teach the Word of God systematically and the other was to do it in the same place over the long haul. I knew that was the only way I could nourish people who would be really doctrinally solid.

Fourth, realize that as you begin to unfold the Scripture, your ministry is going to change. You cannot know everything that the Bible is going to say unless you have dug deeply into it. You may think you have everything wired, but four or five years into your ministry, you will come to a passage that will change the way you think about a certain issue and the way your church does things. You and your people must allow the Word to shape your church.

What is the ultimate key to effective preaching?

Very simply, stay in your study until you know that the Lord will gladly accept what you have prepared to preach because it rightly represents His Word. Let me close with an unforgettable plan suggested by an unknown parishioner as to how to accomplish this.

Fling him into his office. Tear the "Office" sign from the door and nail on the sign, "Study." Take him off the mailing list. Lock him up with his books and his typewriter and his Bible. Slam him down on his knees before texts and broken hearts and the flock of lives of a superficial flock and a holy God.

Force him to be the one man in our surfeited communities who knows about God. Throw him into the ring to box with God until he learns how short his arms are. Engage him to wrestle with God all the night through. And let him come out only when he's bruised and beaten into being a blessing.

Shut his mouth forever spouting remarks, and stop his tongue forever tripping lightly over every nonessential. Require him to have something to say before he dares break the silence. Bend his knees in the lonesome valley.

Burn his eyes with weary study. Wreck his emotional poise with worry for God. And make him exchange his pious stance for a humble walk with God and man. Make him spend and be spent for the glory of God. Rip out his telephone. Burn up his ecclesiastical success sheets.

Put water in his gas tank. Give him a Bible and tie him to the pulpit. And make him preach the Word of the living God!

Test him. Quiz him. Examine him. Humiliate him for his ignorance of things divine. Shame him for his good comprehension of finances, batting averages, and political in-fighting. Laugh at his frustrated effort to play psychiatrist. Form a choir and raise a chant and haunt him with it night and day—"Sir, we would see Jesus."

When at long last he dares assay the pulpit, ask him if he has a word from God. If he does not, then dismiss him. Tell him you can read the morning paper and digest the television commentaries, and think through the day's superficial problems, and manage the community's weary drives, and bless the sordid baked potatoes and green beans, *ad infinitum*, better than he can.

Command him not to come back until he's read and reread, written and rewritten, until he can stand up, worn and forlorn, and say, "Thus saith the Lord."

Break him across the board of his ill-gotten popularity. Smack him hard with his own prestige. Corner him with questions about God. Cover him with demands for celestial wisdom. And give him no escape until he's back against the wall of the Word.

Sit down before him and listen to the only word he has left—God's Word. Let him be totally ignorant of the down-street gossip, but give him a chapter and order him to walk around it, camp on it, sup with it, and come at last to speak it backward and forward, until all he says about it rings with the truth of eternity. When he's burned out by the flaming Word, when he's consumed at last by the fiery grace blazing through him, and when he's privileged to translate the truth of God to man, finally transferred from earth to heaven, then bear him away gently and blow a muted trumpet and lay him down softly. Place a two-edged sword in his coffin, and raise the tomb triumphant. For he was a brave soldier of the Word. And when he died, he had become a man of God." [70]

What should speakers do with their bodies and voices in the delivery of a message to enhance credibility?

How the messenger stands and talks is important because the listeners are going to respond to those gestures. The speaker should consider how he is standing, where he is looking, what he is doing with his hands, how loudly he is speaking, and how he is constructing the messages he is delivering. Eye contact with the audience is important because it helps to build trust between the presenter and the listeners. I try to focus on people individually throughout the congregation. Here is an analogy that might help. If you were going to take a photograph of someone on the right side of the congregation, and you focused in on someone sitting way over to the left-hand side, opened the shutter of your camera and then just turned it around until you got to the right side of the congregation, you wouldn't have a picture. You would have a big blur. If you want focused photographs, you must click the shutter and then with the shutter closed, move, find somebody else; focus on that person and click the shutter again. The first step in enhancing credibility is to make eye-to-eye, emotion-to-emotion,

---

[70] MacArthur, J. 1997, c1992. *Rediscovering expository preaching.* Word Pub.: Dallas

person-to-person contact with his audience. Let me recommend that you try to keep eye contact at all times when speaking to the audience. If you look at your notes to recall what you want to say, pause briefly. If you talk while looking down at your notes rather than at the audience, the message will get lost in the notes.

When I read a text from the pulpit, as I near the end of a sentence, I try to raise my eyes to the audience and deliver the last two or three words from memory. Very often, the ends of sentences are the most significant parts; the powerful words reside there.

The second step to enhancing credibility is to make sure that the voice is strong. Speaking in a quiet tone throughout the message makes the listeners think that you are not sure about what you are saying. A strong voice is a convincing voice. When a speaker increases the volume of his voice, not only does the voice get louder, but it gets fuller. The modulation range expands dramatically, and there's a direct relationship between volume and variation. Instead of relying on a microphone to get additional volume, the presenter should use his own internal energy.

Do you use a personal computer?

The computer has become one of my best friends. My minor in college was Computer Science and I often find myself using those learned skills in the proclamation ministry. Most of my research is done on the computer. My personal laptop is loaded with several study programs such as: Word Search, Power Bible CD, Libronix Digital Library, and Biblical Illustrator. I also use the computer to type my sermon outlines and to store all of my messages preached and taught. When I travel to conventions and revivals, I take my laptop with me. I have found it to be a helpful tool for the trade.

There is no certain time set in stone that should be devoted to the preparation of a message for delivery. The presenter knows what works best for him. Work schedule, family life, and other responsibilities must be taken into consideration. The main thing is that he spends quality time with the Author of the Word and the Word he will deliver.

Epilogue

Sharing the Word of God with purity is both a science and an art. Policies, principles, procedures, and plans are used. This science and art seems to be a lost skill in the preaching and teaching arena today. I am convinced that without the exposition of the Holy Scripture, the preacher/teacher is minimizing the greatness of his calling. The serious student of the Word will be personally challenged to excel and elevate in the proclamation ministry by applying the principles in this training manual. If the presenter of the Word prayerfully follow and faithfully apply the aforementioned principles for presenting the purity of the passage, then the yielded results will be the maintaining of the message and meaning the Master is manifesting throughout the manual known as the Bible. This guide will serve as a valuable and viable tool for those who are sincere and serious about spreading the truth, the whole, truth, and nothing but the truth.

Bibliography

Barbour, G.F., *The Life of Alexander Whyte* (New York: George H. Doran, 1923), 296.

Berkley, J. D. *Preaching to Convince.* "A Leadership/Word book", 1986, Vol. 8.

Bounds, E. M., *Power Through Prayer*, (Grand Rapids:Baker, n.d.), 74.

Burton, Joe W., *Prince of the Pulpit* (Grand Rapids: Zondervan, 1946), 26.

Cameron, Nigel M. and Ferguson, Sinclair B., *Pulpit and People*, [Edinburgh: Rutherford House, 1986].

Catton W.B., *Bruce Catton's Civil War* (New York: Fairfax, 1984).

Ferguson, Sinclair B., *The Holy Spirit,* (Downers Grove, Ill.: InterVarsity Press, 1996), p. 231.

French, R. A. *Diving for pearls in God's treasure chest: An easy way to study the Bible*, Logos, 1999.

Hughes, R. Kent, *Ephesians, The Mystery of the Body of Christ* (Wheaton, Ill.: Crossway, 1990), and *Liberating Ministers from the Success Syndrome* (Wheaton, Ill.: Tyndale, 1987).

Jefferson, Charles Edward, *The Minister As Prophet* (New York: Crowell, 1905), 17.

Kaiser, Walter C., *Toward An Exegetical Theology* (Grand Rapids: Baker, 1981), pp. 7-8, 239.

Larsen, David, *The Anatomy of Preaching*, (Grand Rapids: Baker, 1989), 53–54.

Lloyd-Jones, D. Martyn, *Preaching and Preachers* (Grand Rapids: Zondervan, 1971), 257.

MacArthur, J., Alone *with God*, (Victor Books: Wheaton, Ill., 1995).

MacArthur, J., *Rediscovering Expository Preaching*, (Word Pub.: Dallas, 1997), p.86-87.

MacArthur, J., "The Mandate of Biblical Inerrancy: Expository Preaching," *The Master's Seminary Journal* 1, no. 1 (Spring 1990): 3–15.

Meyer, F. B., *Expository Preaching Plans and Methods* (New York: George H. Duran, 1912), 100.

Moffatt, James, *A Critical and Exegetical Commentary on the Epistle to the Hebrews*, (reprint, Edinburgh: T. & T. Clark, 1968), 158; cf. 156, 192.

Morgan, G. Campbell, *Preaching* (reprint, Grand Rapids: Baker, 1974), 81.

Sangster, William, *The Approach to Preaching* (London: Epworth, 1951), 18.

Shelley, M. 1995. *Changing lives through preaching and worship: 30 strategies for powerful communication*, Library of Christian leadership, Moorings: Nashville, TN).

Sproule, John A., *"Biblical Exegesis and Expository Preaching"* (unpublished lecture at   Grace Theological Seminary, Winona Lake, Ind., 1978), 1.

Sproul, R., Following *Christ*, (Tyndale House Publishers: Wheaton, IL, 1996, c1991).

Spurgeon, H., *Lectures to My Students: Third Series* (reprint, Grand Rapids: Baker, 1977), 2.

The Holy Bible: King James Version. 1995. Logos Research Systems, Inc.: Oak Harbor, WA.

The King James Bible, Thomas Nelson: Nashville,   119, c1982).

Torrey, R. A., *The Power of Prayer and the Prayer of Power*, (New York: Revell, 1924), 35.

Traina, Robert A., *Methodical Bible Study* (Wilmore, Ky.: Author, 1952), 179–80.

Turner, Howard, and N. Turner (1908–76), and A. T. Robertson (1934).

Wiersbe, W. W. & Wiersbe, D., *The Elements of Preaching,* (Tyndale House Publishers: Wheaton, Ill., 1986).

William, J. Rodman, *The Era of the Spirit*, Logos International, 1971.

Unger, Merrill F., *The New Unger's Bible Dictionary* originally published by Moody   Press of Chicago, Illinois. Copyright © 1988. Database © 1997 NavPress Software.

TO THE
HARBOR LIGHT

LIGHTHOUSES OF MARTHA'S VINEYARD,
NANTUCKET, AND CAPE COD

Photographs by ALISON SHAW

Text by Brenda L. Horrigan

Vineyard Stories
Edgartown, Massachusetts

Contents

Foreword

PRETTY PHOTOS OF New England's picturesque lighthouses are far from rare, particularly in this era when so many people have access to high-quality photographic equipment. Lighthouses are pervasive cultural icons, and their beauty draws serious and casual photographers like moths to a flame. But true artistry is rare, and that is why it's such a pleasure to write the foreword for this volume of Alison Shaw's photography.

And what better subjects than the historic lighthouses of Cape Cod, Martha's Vineyard, and Nantucket? This is a widely varied group both in terms of their architecture and their surroundings, from the wind-worn brick tower atop the vibrant clay cliffs at Gay Head to the sturdy cast-iron towers at Nobska, Nauset, and Chatham, from the soft sands of Provincetown to the cozy harbor of Nantucket.

Along with their visual appeal, the lighthouses of the Cape and Islands have a human and technological history that's rich as a bowl of creamy clam chowder. A little historical context might help to deepen our appreciation of the images in this book.

Before there were any lighthouses on Cape Cod, navigation around its long, sandy arm was treacherous. The first recorded European shipwreck on the shores of the east coast of what would become the United States was that of the *Sparrowhawk*, which ran into a sandbar at Nauset Harbor in December 1626. By the late 1700s, more than one hundred ships were rounding the Cape every day.

In 1776, General George Washington proposed a canal through the Cape as a trade route and also to aid military defense. The Continental Congress considered the idea, but it would take more than a century for the canal to become reality.

The U.S. Lighthouse Establishment, created by an act of Congress in 1789, finally took action in 1796, when the government purchased a swath of land on the Highlands of North Truro from a local farmer for the purpose of erecting a lighthouse. It was needed because of a treacherous spot called Peaked Hill Bars, located about a mile northeast of the lighthouse site.

Highland Light, also known as Cape Cod Light, first sent out its beams on November 15, 1797. Its light, one hundred sixty feet above the water, is the highest on the New England mainland. Cape Cod's first lighthouse keeper was Isaac Small, the farmer who had sold his land to the government. In recognition of the fact that Small had to wind the light's rotating mechanism twice each night, his salary was eventually raised from $150 to $200 yearly.

Henry David Thoreau, a man who famously appreciated life on the border between civilization and nature, visited Highland Light several times between 1849 and 1857. He wrote about spending a night in the keeper's house in his book *Cape Cod*:

I thought as I lay there, half awake and half asleep, looking upward through the window at the lights above my head, how many sleepless eyes from far out on the Ocean stream—mariners of all nations spinning their yarns through the various watches of the night—were directed toward my couch.

Before Cape Cod's second light station was established in 1808 at Chatham, mariners talked of a ghostly rider on a white horse who appeared on stormy nights, swinging a lantern that lured ships to their doom. Chatham originally received two lighthouses, in an effort to make the station easy to distinguish from the single light at North Truro.

Shipping volume increased through the nineteenth century. Josiah Hardy, longtime lighthouse keeper at Chatham, reported an incredible 16,000 vessels passing his station during daylight hours in 1875. On a single day in the 1880s, he counted 365 barks, brigs, schooners, and other ships rounding the Cape's elbow.

More stations followed Highland and Chatham: Race Point at Provincetown (1816), Point Gammon at the entrance to the harbor of Hyannis (1816), Sandy Neck at Barnstable (1826), and the Three Sisters of Nauset at Eastham (1838). Eventually, a total of eighteen light stations would be established on Cape Cod and in nearby waters.

The lighthouse history of Nantucket reaches back even further than Cape Cod's. By the 1740s, Nantucket's celebrated whaling industry was booming. At a town meeting in January 1746, local merchants and mariners voted to erect a lighthouse at Brant Point to mark the point around which all vessels passed as they entered the island's harbor.

Brant Point Light was the second light station in North America, after Boston Light (1716). An astounding total of nine different lighthouse structures have stood at Brant Point over the years, not including a bonfire on a hogshead (barrel) that was said to be in use as early as 1700. The short but picturesque wooden tower that now stands at the point was erected in 1901.

Nantucket boasts two other scenic lighthouses, at Great Point (established 1784) and Sankaty Head (established 1850). The present tower at Great Point, the northernmost reach of the "Gray Lady," is actually a 1986 reproduction constructed after a brutal March storm reduced its predecessor to a pile of rubble.

When the lighthouse at Sankaty Head on Nantucket's southeast coast was established in 1850, it was given a powerful second-order Fresnel lens, called a "blazing star" by the historian Samuel Adams Drake. As Nantucket evolved from whaling capital to vacation resort, the lighthouse became a popular attraction.

The lighthouse legacy of Martha's Vineyard dates to 1799 with the establishment of the Gay Head Light at the western extremity of the island. The initial keeper, Ebenezer Skiff, was the first white man to live in the vicinity, which was populated by Wampanoag Indians. Charles Vanderhoop, a Wampanoag Indian, became one of the light's most popular keepers.

The lights are all automated now, and traditional lighthouse keeping is a thing of the past. Today's keepers are the preservationists, with organizations like the Martha's Vineyard Museum and the American Lighthouse Foundation working to preserve these coastal treasures and their associated history. I urge anyone who's derived a moment's pleasure from a lighthouse to consider donating, or perhaps volunteering his or her time, to one of the lighthouse preservation organizations.

The artist Jamie Wyeth, who lives at a lighthouse in Maine, has said that he could spend three lifetimes at his island home and not scratch the surface of subjects for his paintings. Alison Shaw brings a comparable artist's eye to her lighthouse photography. As with any outstanding artist, her work makes us feel like we're looking at these structures for the first time. Her strikingly original work stands out like a beacon in a sea of cliché.

Jeremy D'Entremont
Portsmouth, New Hampshire
February 2012

Martha's Vineyard

SOME CALL LIGHTHOUSES "castles by the sea," but lighthouses are not stone fortresses erected to protect those within. Rather, they look out, and reach out. They are reflections of a spirit forged in an age when character, noble purpose, and duty were the ballast of a worthy life.

Gay Head Light, a tower of salt- and sand-smoothed red brick, rises up from the clay cliffs of Aquinnah and overlooks the convoy of history, the seafaring trail forged by explorers and settlers, whalers, traders, and immigrants.

The first keeper of Cape Poge Lighthouse raised eight children on a desolate, low-lying beach, and sheltered shipwreck victims, often for days. Lighthouse keepers endured harsh conditions and, at times, serious deprivation. They ran newly trimmed and filled lamps up and down the spiraling stair on the most bone-chill winter nights. They cared for others before themselves.

No less could be said of the West Chop and Edgartown keepers, though these two lights were heralds to the busy harbors of Vineyard Haven and Edgartown. Looking out from either today, you are reminded less of underwater hazards and shipwrecks and more of those days when a ship's arrival drew excited townsfolk to the wharf to reunite with family members or marvel as exotic wares from far-off lands were unloaded.

In East Chop the spirit of duty and fellowship was evoked in another way. While federal officials mulled over whether the Vineyard really needed a fifth lighthouse, locals rallied to ensure the safety of sea travelers. Locals ran a semaphore system until a sea captain collected funds to build a modest light. In 1880, the government at last approved the cast-iron, brick-lined tower that stands today.

MARTHA'S VINEYARD LIGHTHOUSES: Cape Poge, East Chop, Edgartown, Gay Head, West Chop

Cape Poge

In December 1801, Matthew Mayhew, appointed keeper by President Thomas Jefferson, lit the Vineyard's second lighthouse. In the next century, only the English Channel had more shipping traffic; thirty thousand ships passed through Vineyard waters in the year 1844–45 alone. Cape Poge was, as an 1838 naval inspector succinctly put it, "an exceedingly useful light."

American lighthouses were extinguished during the War of 1812. In 1814, fearing a British invasion, Keeper Matthew Mayhew hauled the lamp and other equipment to a Chappaquiddick basement. The lighthouse was relit the following year. A decade later Mayhew feared another enemy: erosion. Already half of the original four acres of lighthouse property had disappeared. Eventually the lighthouse structures fell into the sea. The present tower, a "temporary" structure built in 1893, has since been moved three times, most recently in 1987.

East Chop

Beginning in the early 1800s, while Congress ignored pleas for a second lighthouse at Vineyard Haven Harbor, local residents made do with a semaphore system, using flags and hand signals to warn approaching ships of coastal hazards. Naturally, this was of little use at night, so lanterns were also rigged, paid for either with private funds or a tax on merchants transporting wares by sea. Government gridlock was at last broken, and the East Chop Lighthouse lit, in 1878.

The light source beaming from the forty-foot, cast-iron tower on Oak Bluff's Telegraph Hill is a 300mm optic, but originally the lighthouse contained a fourth-order Fresnel lens. French physicist Augustin Fresnel invented his lens in 1822, placing prisms in a precise, beehive-like arrangement. The largest Fresnels, called hyper-radial, first-order, and second-order, were intended for major lighthouses (like Gay Head). Smaller sizes, which go from third to sixth in the United States but higher in Europe, were assigned to harbor entrances and less critical spots.

Change came to East Chop in 1933 when the lamp was automated, and the beacon was changed from flashing red to flashing green. Following extensive renovations in the late 1980s, the grounds were open to the public in 1990.

Edgartown

Built in 1828, the first lighthouse at Edgartown was set on wooden pilings at the Point of Flats, near the harbor entrance. Funds allotted by Congress, though, were insufficient to build a pier connecting the lighthouse to shore; the first keeper was forced to row to work. A causeway was built in 1830, but ice swept away much of it the first winter. Below, renowned Vineyard painter Ray Ellis, whose art is closely associated with coastal Edgartown locations, captures the lighthouse on canvas.

When the hurricane of 1938 hit, the original tower was already in bad shape.
The Coast Guard dismantled it and replaced it with a forty-five-foot cast-iron
tower brought by barge from Crane's Beach in Ipswich.

Gay Head

When it was rebuilt in 1856, Gay Head Light also received a first-order Fresnel lens, one of the largest sizes made and containing 1,008 prisms. While many East Coast lighthouses stayed lit during World War II, Gay Head was dimmed. As the daughter of the keeper of the nearby Cuttyhunk Lighthouse put it, "They didn't want to help the Germans *that* much." The Fresnel is now on display at the Martha's Vineyard Museum.

West Chop

Congress approved a third Vineyard lighthouse in 1817. A twenty-five-foot tower of stone put the lantern sixty feet above sea level, at the time sufficient to warn ships attempting to reach Vineyard Haven Harbor of the threat from the Squash Meadow and Norton's Shoals. By the 1890s, construction of tall homes in the increasingly popular resort area eventually required that a taller tower be built.

West Chop Light has been rebuilt and relocated several times, due to construction problems and shore erosion. In 1856–57, in a wave of U.S. government lighthouse retrofitting, West Chop's old reflector lamp was replaced with a fourth-order Fresnel lens, which remains in place today. The current tower, forty-five feet tall, was built in 1891. The U.S. Coast Guard now manages the property.

Nantucket

NANTUCKET ISLAND IS made largely of sand and surrounded by broad, shifting shoals. Navigational charts were of marginal use to the thousands of ships stopping here during colonial times. Thus, in 1746 the island got its first light, the nation's second—Brant Point in Nantucket Harbor.

In 1784 a second lighthouse, also a harbor guide, was built at Great Point, the southern edge of what was once America's busiest sea passage. Built in 1850, Sankaty Head, near the town of Siasconset, warned mariners away from the shoals of the island's southern shore.

While all three lights remain active, ships today do have modern means by which to navigate. Yet Nantucket's three lighthouses have been carefully preserved, rebuilt, even moved at great expense. Why bother to preserve lighthouses? What purpose do they serve?

A lighthouse is more than a navigational tool. It's a monument and a reminder.

The view from a lighthouse tower reminds us there remain many unknown places to explore. An examination of the lamp and service rooms recalls the proud and self-sufficient keepers who sacrificed so that passing strangers would be safe.

A lighthouse is a memento of a quieter, more intimate era—before computers and television. A time when people relied on each other for companionship and entertainment. A time when the sight of a neighbor, friend, or family member returning home was a cause for celebration.

Lighthouses recall to us the true essentials of a good life.

NANTUCKET LIGHTHOUSES: Brant Point, Great Point, Sankaty Head

Even in the colonial era, Nantucket was one of the East Coast's major ports and the hub of its whaling industry. Lives and vast fortunes depended on safe passage in and out of Nantucket Harbor, so in 1746, the citizens at the town meeting voted to construct a lighthouse, the American colonies' second, after Boston.

At least nine structures have borne the name Brant Point Light—poor construction, accidental fires, and freak wind gusts have made it our nation's most-often *rebuilt* lighthouse. Over the generations its style and location have changed, as improved construction techniques were adopted or the sandy harbor channels shifted. The present light dates from 1901 (its 1856 predecessor still stands, just down the road).

Great Point

Nantucket's second lighthouse (sometimes called Nantucket Light), Great Point sits on the island's northern tip. A lighthouse was first proposed for this site in colonial times, but no action taken before the Revolutionary War began. It was at last built and lit in 1784. The first keeper, Captain Paul Pinkham, was also the first to draw an accurate map of the shoals off shore, though ships continued to wreck there, the underwater hazards being so numerous in these busy Atlantic waters.

Originally a wooden tower, Great Point burned down twice before being rebuilt as a stone structure in 1818; a brick lining was added in 1857, the same year a Fresnel lens was installed. A hurricane in 1984 turned the tower into a pile of rubble overnight. It was rebuilt two years later. Today it's part of the Coskata-Coatue Wildlife Refuge, a place popular with both naturalists and saltwater anglers, who come in search of striped bass and bluefish.

Sankaty Head

The English word *window* comes from two Old Norse words: *vindr* (wind) and *auga* (eye). To look out from the lamp room's windows, one hundred fifty feet above the sea, is to indeed look the wind in the eye. From this perch, the keepers of Sankaty Head watched whaling captains and crews voyage off on years-long hunts. When the mariners turned back for home they watched the horizon, no doubt yearning for sight of what they called "the blazing star," for this lighthouse, built in 1850, was the first in America with a Fresnel lens as part of its original equipment.

Cape Cod

HAD FRENCH EXPLORER Samuel de Champlain arrived first, Cape Cod might now be Cap Mal-Barre (Cape Bad-Sandbar). But British captain Bartholomew Gosnold landed four years earlier, and was more taken with the codfish-rich waters. Still, Champlain's wariness of the Cape's underwater ledges, rocks, and shoals was warranted; the hazards of rounding the Cape plagued so many sailors that, over eighty-three years, eighteen lighthouse towers rose up to serve as day marks and night beacons.

Lighthouses reach up, but they also reach out. The presence of so many black-hatted light towers dotting their coast reinforced the Cape community's outward focus, and its particularly selfless compassion for the strangers traveling just off their shores. Lighthouse keepers (and their families—wives and children also hauled oil, trimmed wicks, and stood watch) were renowned for their vigilance. And when they raised the alarm, neighbors rushed to their boats to try to reach a shipwreck's victims. (Thoreau wrote of reading in his newspaper about a wreck, and sometimes a dozen, after every Cape Cod storm. "The inhabitants hear the crash of vessels going to pieces as they sit round their hearths.")

Cape Cod lighthouses recall the heroism of everyday people generations ago, when crossing the sea, or just rounding the Cape, meant risking one's life. That drama remains palpable today. Set at sea level, in towns still devoid of vertical structures, the towers soar up into the open sky. Today, standing in a lighthouse tower is a chance to see that sea anew, and remember that it is vast and that there's much left for us each to explore.

- -

CAPE COD LIGHTHOUSES: Chatham, Highland, Lewis Bay, Long Point, Monomoy, Nauset, Nobska Point, Race Point, Sandy Neck, Stage Harbor, Wings Neck, Wood End

Chatham Light marks one corner of the hazardous triangle formed with Highland Light and Pollock's Rip. The *Mayflower* was forced to turn back to Provincetown after it attempted to enter the area. Between 1843 and 1959, over a thousand wrecks were recorded in the region.

Cape Cod's second lighthouse, Chatham was lit in 1808. Originally, it was two towers—"the Twins"—to distinguish it from the Highland Light. When the builder arrived from off-Cape to construct the towers, he was startled to find that the native rock he'd planned to use was nowhere to be found on the Cape's sandy plain. The wooden towers he constructed quickly decayed in the salt air. They were replaced with brick towers and eventually with cast-iron, brick-lined structures. Love of their local lighthouse is common among Cape Codders; on New Year's Eve it's a tradition here to gather for a town group photo, shown here.

Highland

Henry David Thoreau remarked on the multitude of official regulations and directives the keepers were required to obey, some of which he found ridiculous. For example, a keeper was expected to record the number of passing ships. But here, said Thoreau, "there are a hundred vessels in sight at once, steering in all directions, many on the very verge of the horizon, and he must have more eyes than Argus and be a great deal farther sighted to tell which are passing his light."

The "fanged" coast of Cape Cod was a hazard to mariners from the arrival of the earliest explorers. After intense lobbying by seafaring Bostonians, the Cape got its first lighthouse in 1797 in Truro. A wooden structure, it was replaced by a brick tower in 1831 and then, in 1857, with the cast-iron tower that stands today. With a 170-foot focal plane, Highland is the highest light on the New England mainland.

Lewis Bay

Several lighthouses on the Cape were, initially at least, constructed privately. Lewis Bay Light is a replica of Nantucket's Brant Point Light. This Hyannis Harbor landmark serves as a handsome daymark and flashes a green light at night for passing ferries. Because it is private and not officially recognized by the U.S. Coast Guard, this light has no official name. In addition to Lewis Bay, some call it the Hyannis Inner Harbor Light or Channel Point Light.

Long Point

When first lit in 1826, the second light by Provincetown's harbor was in a bustling community with a schoolhouse and a saltworks. (In *Cape Cod Pilot*, Josef Berger wrote with evident amusement that children who in other villages might be wary of stray dogs instead "ran from" the sharks trolling the waters off Provincetown.) The settlement shrank in the 1850s and by the time of the Civil War, few people still remained; many village buildings were floated by boat to Provincetown's West End.

The original lighthouse was a lantern atop the keeper's house. The current tower, square-shaped and built of brick, was erected in 1875 and included a fifth-order Fresnel lens. Long Point's modern optic has been solar-powered since 1982.

Monomoy

In 1770, Monomoy was a peninsula; by 1800, it had become an island. It is in flux still, one of the rare places where the beach between the tower and sea is growing. First lit in 1823, the tower was painted red in 1882 to improve its daymark capability. Iron trusses were added a decade later to strengthen it against the wind. Today it is part of Monomoy National Wildlife Refuge, famed for the variety of birdlife.

Nauset

Nauset's first lighthouse was lit in 1838. The current forty-eight-foot tower was originally one of "the Twins" at Chatham Light, moved here in 1918. In 1996, professional house movers were hired to again relocate this tower, bringing it inland and away from the eroding shoreline. Nauset Light is today part of the Cape Cod National Seashore. It operates as a private aid to navigation.

One of the oldest recorded shipwrecks off the Cape occurred near here in 1717 when pirate captain "Black Sam" Bellamy's vessel went down with twenty thousand pounds of gold and silver aboard it had just taken from a slave-trading ship. Accounts vary on what happened to the crew members who survived—some say they were promptly hanged in Eastham, others that they went on trial in Boston. Undersea explorer Barry Clifford discovered the wreckage and its booty in 1984.

Nobska Point

The first light here, lit in 1829, was a lantern constructed atop the keeper's house. It proved to be a poor design; the stress on the house rafters made the roof leak. The current tower offers a 240-degree view; its red glass panel is set so that ships approaching are warned in ample time to correct course and avoid dangerous underwater shoals.

Lighthouse keepers were known as "wick trimmers," or "wickies." The playful term belies the demanding nature of the job. In addition to tending the light every night and watching for mariners in distress, keepers and their families were subject to white-glove inspections. Here, Michael Bedard wears an authentic nineteenth-century keeper's uniform; he is a member of the Coast Guard Auxiliary, which today keeps the lighthouse polished and ready for its two thousand annual visitors.

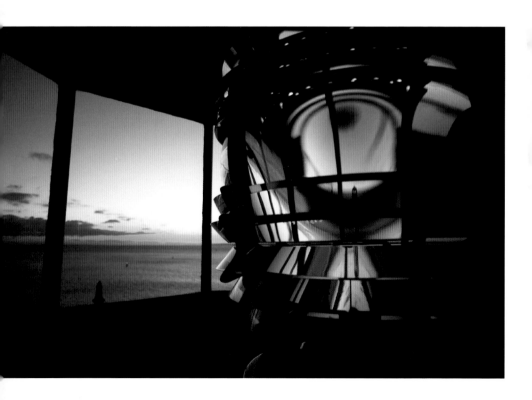

Race Point

Until 1914, when the Cape Cod Canal opened, seafaring traffic between Boston and points south passed Race Point. Thus, it was the natural location for the Cape's third lighthouse, which was lit in 1816. Made of rubblestone and lime mortar, equipped with one of the first revolving lights, it warned mariners away from the treacherous Peaked Hill Bars. Bones from eighteenth-century wrecks are still to be found in these waters off Provincetown.

The remoteness of Race Point meant a harsh life for lighthouse keepers and their families. The children of the keeper hiked over two miles through sand to get to school. By horse, it was a seventy-five-minute trip. But in 1935 keeper James Hinckley used a Ford with soft tires, which turned it into a half-hour excursion. Some call this the first "dune buggy."

Sandy Neck

After the lighthouse was decommissioned, its lantern room was removed; the Coast Guard was concerned sun might reflect off the room's glass and confuse sailors. In 2007 the family that owns the property, working with the Cape Cod Chapter of the American Lighthouse Foundation, had a replica lantern installed. Sandy Neck was relit in 2007. With a high-power LED lantern visible for thirteen miles, it is again an aid to navigation.

Stage Harbor

Explorer Samuel de Champlain lost a rudder near here in the 1600s. Later mariners benefited from the lighthouse built in 1880, the third in Chatham. But by the 1930s, with the drop in seafaring traffic and changes in the shoreline, it was deemed unnecessary—much to the consternation of its keeper, who was thus put out of work in the midst of the Great Depression. In 1933, the lantern was removed and the property auctioned off. It remains a private residence and "headless."

One of America's most commended lighthouse keepers lived at Stage Harbor. Alfred A. Howard, who served during 1906–1916, was recognized for towing in a catboat that ran out of fuel (1912), for guiding a stranded yacht whose owner didn't know the waters (1912), and for saving a man whose dory overturned (1913). The U.S. Secretary of Commerce personally acknowledged Howard's 1914 rescue of a horse stuck in sand that otherwise would have drowned.

Wings Neck

In the 1800s, this Pocasset peninsula in Buzzard's Bay was a busy site thanks to commercial traffic from several nearby iron foundries. The first lighthouse was a tower atop a keeper's house, lit in 1849. A new house, with a separate hexagonal tower replaced it in 1890.

Wings Neck has its share of interesting historical notes. A keeper in the 1850s, John Maxim died at the Battle of Gettysburg. In the 1920s, when President Warren G. Harding's boat anchored offshore because of bad weather, keeper Wallace Eldredge used his foghorn to deliver his version of a twenty-one-gun salute. The lighthouse even played host to the von Trapp family singers after it was decommissioned in 1947 and sold to the musically inclined Flanagan family of Boston.

During the Civil War, two forts were hastily built in anticipation of a Confederate attack by sea. They were never used, but instead became the site of Provincetown's third lighthouse, lit in 1873. The square-shaped tower of white-painted brick originally contained a fourth-order Fresnel lens but since 1981 has held a solar-powered aero-beacon. In 1911 a stone breakwater was built to protect Provincetown harbor; it allows visitors to walk to the lighthouse at low tide, an excursion that takes over an hour one way.

MARTHA'S VINEYARD

Cape Poge Light

Description: Located at the northeast corner of the island of Chappaquiddick within the Trustees of Reservations Cape Poge Wildlife Refuge. Owned and operated by the U.S. Coast Guard and managed by the Trustees.

Access: The best way to see the lighthouse (and the only way to see the interior) is via the Trustees' over-sand guided vehicle tours. Also accessible via private four-wheel-drive vehicle with an over-sand permit or by foot on a seven-mile round-trip hike over sand.

Info: The Trustees of Reservations, 508-627-3599.

East Chop Light

Description: Located on the tip of East Chop at the entrance to Vineyard Haven Harbor. Owned and operated by the U.S. Coast Guard and managed by the Martha's Vineyard Museum.

Access: Easily accessible and open to the public in season on a limited basis. Free for museum members. A small fee is charged for nonmembers.

Info: Martha's Vineyard Museum, 508-627-4441, www.mvmuseum.org.

Edgartown Light

Description: Located at the entrance to Edgartown Harbor. Owned and operated by the U.S. Coast Guard and managed by the Martha's Vineyard Museum.

Access: Sweeping view from the end of North Water Street, and the lighthouse is an easy five-minute walk from the street. Open to the public daily in the summer months and in the late spring and early fall on a limited basis. Free for museum members. A small fee is charged for nonmembers.

Info: Martha's Vineyard Museum, 508-627-4441, www.mvmuseum.org.

Gay Head Light

Description: Perched atop the Gay Head Cliffs in the town of Aquinnah at the far western end of the island. Owned and operated by the U.S. Coast Guard and managed by the Martha's Vineyard Museum.

Access: Easily accessible. The best view is from the viewing area beyond the shops and restaurants at the Gay Head Cliffs. The lighthouse and grounds are open to the public daily in the summer months, and in the late spring and early fall on a limited basis. Free for museum members. A small fee is charged for nonmembers.

Info: Martha's Vineyard Museum, 508-627-4441, www.mvmuseum.org.

Note: The original first-order Fresnel lens from this lighthouse is on the grounds of the Martha's Vineyard Museum.

West Chop Light

Description: Located on the tip of West Chop at the entrance to Vineyard Haven Harbor. Owned and operated by the U.S. Coast Guard.

Access: Easily viewed from the road but closed to the public.

NANTUCKET
Brant Point Light
Description: Located on the beach at the entrance to Nantucket Harbor. Owned and operated by the U.S. Coast Guard.

Access: There's a great view of the lighthouse from the ferry as you enter Nantucket Harbor. It is an easy walk or drive from town, at the end of Easton Street. Grounds are open, but the interior is not.

Note: The fourth-order Fresnel lens from the lighthouse is on display at the Nantucket Shipwreck and Lifesaving Museum.

Great Point Light
Description: Located at the northernmost point of Nantucket Island. Owned and operated by the U.S. Coast Guard and located within the U.S. Fish and Wildlife Service Nantucket National Wildlife Refuge. The Trustees of Reservations Coskata-Coatue Wildlife Refuge is just to the south of the lighthouse. The Trustees manage the lighthouse.

Access: The best way to see the lighthouse is on one of the Trustees' over-sand guided vehicle tours, which generally operate daily in season. (There are many days when the tours do not reach the lighthouse for various reasons, including nesting shorebirds.) The only way to view the interior of the lighthouse tower is on a Trustees tour. There is a fee for the tours.

The lighthouse is accessible via private four-wheel-drive vehicle with an over-sand permit. Several Jeep rental agencies on Nantucket rent Jeeps; pay the day-pass fee at the Wauwinet Gatehouse. Access the lighthouse free on foot, but it is a very challenging twelve-mile round-trip hike over sand.

Info: The Wauwinet Gatehouse, 508-228-6799 for information or to book a tour.

Note: The third-order Fresnel lens from the lighthouse is on display on the grounds of the Nantucket Shipwreck and Lifesaving Museum.

Sankaty Head Light
Description: Located on a bluff at the far eastern end of Nantucket on the outskirts of the village of Siasconset. Owned and maintained by the 'Sconset Trust. Private aid to navigation.

Access: Easily accessible. The interior is open to the public at no charge in the spring during Nantucket Preservation Month and on Columbus Day weekend.

Info: 'Sconset Trust, 508-228-9917, www.sconsettrust.org.

Note: The second-order Fresnel lens from the lighthouse is on display at the Nantucket Historical Association Whaling Museum.

CAPE COD
Bass River (West Dennis) Light
Description: Atop the Lighthouse Inn in West Dennis, overlooking Nantucket Sound. Bass River Light is a U.S. Coast Guard–sanctioned, privately owned, and privately maintained lighthouse. It is lit May through October.

Access: Viewed from the grounds of the inn and accessed from the interior of the inn.

Info: Lighthouse Inn, www.lighthouseinn.com.

Chatham Light
Description: Located overlooking Chatham Harbor and Lighthouse Beach. Owned and operated by the U.S. Coast Guard.

Access: There is a clear view of the lighthouse from the road, but the grounds are open only during tours offered by the local Coast Guard Auxiliary. During July and August public tours are each Wednesday afternoon. There are additional open hours during spring and fall and again on New Year's Eve.

Info: U.S. Coast Guard Auxiliary website.

Note: The tower's original lantern room and fourth-order Fresnel lens are on display at the Atwood House Museum

Highland (Cape Cod) Light

Description: In North Truro on a high bluff overlooking the Atlantic Ocean. Owned by the Cape Cod National Seashore and maintained and operated by the Highland Museum and Lighthouse Inc. The U.S. Coast Guard maintains the light itself.

Access: The lighthouse and gift shop are open to the public every day in season, off-season tours by appointment (there is a forty-eight-inch height requirement for children to climb the tower). There is a small fee to visit the lighthouse.

Info: Highland Museum and Lighthouse, 508-487-1121, www.capecodlight.org.

Lewis Bay Light

Description: Located at the entrance to Hyannis Harbor. Privately owned and is a replica of the Brant Point Light on Nantucket. Not an active aid to navigation.

Access: It prominently anchors the entrance to Hyannis Harbor, and the ferries to Nantucket and the Vineyard travel directly past it. By land, it is most easily viewed across the harbor from the end of Pleasant Street. At the end of Daisy Hill Road, there is a public right-of-way to the small beach adjoining the property where the lighthouse is located—the lighthouse itself is surrounded by private property.

Long Point Light

Description: Located at the very tip of Cape Cod, at the entrance to Provincetown Harbor. Owned by the U.S. Coast Guard and maintained by the Cape Cod Chapter of the American Lighthouse Foundation.

Access: The easiest way to view from a reasonable distance is aboard the many whale watching or sightseeing trips departing from Provincetown Harbor daily in season.

On foot, the 5.5-mile round-trip walk is challenging. Begin with a forty-five-minute walk at low tide along the breakwater that crosses the far end of the harbor. The rocks on the breakwater are uneven and difficult to traverse. Once across, turn left toward the lighthouse. Walk to the lighthouse on the harbor side of Long Point and back on the ocean side for a change of scenery.

The lighthouse is an easy kayak paddle across the harbor. Flyer's Boat Yard rents kayaks and provides an hourly shuttle service from MacMillan Pier to Long Point in season.

Info: Flyer's Boat Yard, www.flyersrentals.com.

Monomoy Light

Description: Located in the Monomoy National Wildlife Refuge, on South Monomoy, off the coast of Chatham. Owned by the U.S. Fish and Wildlife Service. Not an active aid to navigation.

Access: The Monomoy Island Ferry offers day trips to Monomoy National Wildlife Refuge for a fee, departing from refuge headquarters on Morris Island in Chatham. The walking tours on Monomoy are led by a naturalist and can include a visit to the lighthouse.

Also accessible by private boat to Monomoy or a challenging nineteen-mile round-trip walk. Start your walk from Lighthouse Beach.

Info: Monomoy National Wildlife Refuge, 508-945-0594, www.fws.gov/northeast/monomoy. The Monomoy Island Ferry, 508-237-0420, www.monomoyislandferry.com.

Nauset Light

Description: Located near Nauset Light Beach in Eastham. Owned by the National Park Service and maintained and operated by the Nauset Light Preservation Society (NLPS).

Access: The NLPS provides public tours of Nauset Light on Sundays, May through late October, and also on Wednesdays during July and August.

Info: NLPS, www.nausetlight.org.

Nobska Point Light

Description: Located high on a dramatic point of land, overlooking the village of Woods Hole, Vineyard Sound, and the Island of Martha's Vineyard. Owned and operated by the U.S. Coast Guard.

Access: Easily viewed from the road, and the grounds are open to the public. The tower is open for occasional tours conducted by the local Coast Guard Auxiliary.

Info: U.S. Coast Guard Auxiliary website.

Point Gammon Light

Description: Located to the east of the entrance to Hyannis Harbor, on the southern tip of West Yarmouth's Great Island. Privately owned, and not an active aid to navigation.

Access: No public access. There is a distant view of the lighthouse from the ferries travelling from Hyannis to Nantucket and Martha's Vineyard.

Race Point Light

Description: Located in the Cape Cod National Seashore at the far end of Provincetown. Owned by the U.S. Coast Guard and maintained by the Cape Cod Chapter of the American Lighthouse Foundation.

Access: Periodically open for tours during the spring, summer, and fall months. The keeper's house and whistle house are both available for overnight guests.

Accessible via private four-wheel-drive vehicle with an Off Road Vehicle (ORV) permit issued by the Cape Cod National Seashore. Art's Dune Tours offers over-sand tours out to the lighthouse. If you are spending the night at the lighthouse, transportation is provided.

The walk to the lighthouse is 3.4 miles round-trip from the Race Point Beach parking lot—you can follow the ORV road or walk on the beach. An alternative is to go to Herring Cove Beach and walk down the beach to your right—at low tide you can walk all the way to the lighthouse, traversing the shallow waters at the entrance to Hatches Harbor.

Info: For lighthouse tours or lodging, call 508-487-9930, or on the web at www.racepointlighthouse.net. Art's Dune Tours, 508-487-1950, www.artsdunetours.com.

Sandy Neck Light

Description: Located on Sandy Neck Beach at the entrance to Barnstable Harbor. Sandy Neck Beach is a conservation and recreation area owned by the town of Barnstable. The keeper's house and the lighthouse are privately owned, and the lighthouse is maintained by the Sandy Neck Lighthouse Restoration Committee as a private aid to navigation.

Access: The lighthouse is on private property with no public access. Reachable by four-wheel-drive vehicle with an Off Road Vehicle permit from the town of Barnstable. You can walk to the lighthouse, but it is a twelve-mile round-trip walk over sand.

The lighthouse can be viewed from a distance across Barnstable Harbor at Millway Beach. The beach is also an easy spot to launch a kayak, if you'd like to paddle across Barnstable Harbor to get a closer look.

South Hyannis Light

Description: Located in a residential neighborhood in Hyannis, and not an active aid to navigation.

Access: The lighthouse and grounds are privately owned and not open to the public but can be viewed from the end of Harbor Road.

Stage Harbor Light

Description: Located at the entrance to Stage Harbor in Chatham. Not an active aid to navigation.

Access: The lighthouse and grounds are privately owned, but it is an easy two-mile round-trip walk from Hardings Beach for a closer look. There is also a nice view of the lighthouse across Stage Harbor from the Stage Harbor Yacht Club.

Tarpaulin Cove Light

Description: Located on the shores of Naushon Island, overlooking Vineyard Sound. The island is privately owned. The lighthouse is owned and operated by the U.S. Coast Guard and maintained by the Cuttyhunk Historical Society.

Access: No public access to the island or the lighthouse except on a one-day open house sponsored by the historical society and usually in early August.

The lighthouse can also be viewed from the water by private boat. Tarpaulin Cove is a favorite anchorage for boaters.

Info: Cuttyhunk Historical Society, www.cuttyhunkhistoricalsociety.org.

Three Sisters Lights

Description: Located in a park setting just inland from Nauset Light Beach. Owned by the National Park Service and maintained by the Cape Cod National Seashore. Not an active aid to navigation.

Access: A short walk west on Cable Road from the Nauset Light Beach parking lot. There are weekly tours of the lighthouses in season.

Info: Salt Pond Visitors Center, 508-255-3421.

Wings Neck Light

Description: Located on private property on Wings Neck Point, with a high, sweeping view of Buzzard's Bay. Not an active aid to navigation.

Access: Easily viewed from the road, but there is no public parking. The lighthouse and keeper's house are available for weekly rentals.

Info: www.wingsnecklighthouse.com.

Wood End Light

Description: Located at the southernmost point of the sandy hook that forms Provincetown Harbor. Owned by the U.S. Coast Guard and maintained by the Cape Cod Chapter of the American Lighthouse Foundation.

Access: The three-mile round-trip walk to the lighthouse starts at the harbor breakwater (go at low tide). Once you reach the other side, turn right and head for the lighthouse.